Growing Up Carlisle

"A Wonderful Mid-America Childhood In The 50's & 60's"

Jim Garnett

Foreword By Susan Randleman-Robinson

Copyright © Jim Garnett 2014
Ziklag Publishers

Foreword

Growing up in Carlisle during the 50's and 60's was relatively uncomplicated. Those of us who were blessed to experience this time and place in our life, weren't aware of it then, but now as we wistfully look back, we realize that it was truly a magical time.

Since Jim and I grew up in Carlisle during the same era of time, I have memories of some the same things he shares in the book, like going to fires in Carlisle, Sunday afternoon drives, the Carlisle 4th, and all the childhood fads that came and went. And I too have fond recollections of my brother and I walking to the bottom of Lindhardt Road and sitting on the big rock that used to be at the foot of the hill. Just like Jim, we shared the same simple ritual of meeting our Dad when he returned from work.

This book made me smile as it took me back to the nostalgia of my own childhood memories and allowed me to relive them once again. I even found myself jotting down those memories so I could share them with my kids and grandkids.

Jim has an unusual conversational style of writing that makes it seem as if he is talking to you as he relates, in his witty way, his humorous and charming recollections. His memoirs are both funny and entertaining.

You will find, like I did, that there is something pleasurable and peaceful about taking a trip down memory lane and stopping for a moment to recapturing those long lost remembrances!

Susan Randleman-Robinson

2

Introduction

I was born in Carlisle, Iowa, in 1949, and lived there until I graduated from high school in 1968. I never gave much thought about the details of growing up in Carlisle until I received a copy of a book entitled "Depot Street Memories: The Lawler Stories" by Bill Sheridan (you can get it on Kindle or Nook). The book is an interesting collection of Mr. Sheridan's memories about growing up in Lawler, Iowa, in the 1950's.

As I read through the chapters of his book, his childhood memories began to "jumpstart" my own childhood memories! Even though the details of his childhood were different than mine, the small town setting was the same, and the time era was the same. I found myself reading a chapter or two of his book, then stopping to jot down notes about the memories that were stirred up inside me.

Memories are a funny thing. I think a person's memories are stored in little "boxes" in our brains somewhere. The boxes are similar to the little mailboxes families had at the Carlisle Post Office when I was a child. The walls were lined with row-after-row of these mailboxes, each with its own combination. Inside was that family's mail for the day.

Each memory box has its own combination, and is filled with all the sights, sounds, smells, tastes, and feelings connected with that specific memory.

The combination that opens the box might be something we see, hear, taste, smell, or even feel. When the memory box opens, everything inside of it spills out, whether pleasant or unpleasant, and for a brief moment we relive the memory. Mr. Sheridan's book was full of memories that worked like "combinations" to unlock memory boxes in my mind. That produced for me a very enjoyable trip to the past as I remembered scenes that I had not thought about for many years.

Me At Age 2

I hope to create a similar experience for you. I want my memories to be the "combinations" which will unlock your memory boxes so you can relive and enjoy those experiences once again. My memories are just that –memories. They are factual *as I remember them* but that is through the eyes of a little boy.

I found, as I hope you will, that my childhood memories took me back to a pleasant and peaceful time where life was safe, secure, and satisfying.

They took me back to a time when responsibility and pressure were virtually unknown, a time when the pursuit of living life to the fullest was the priority of the day, and a time when the "lens" that focused the world around me was the eyes of a child. As they say, "Those were the days!"

If this book can help you remember and relax, while your mind takes a few "minute vacations," I have been a success and my goal has been accomplished.

Sincerely,

Jim Garnett

Table Of Contents

Chapter One

Fire, Fire!

One of the most exciting events in Carlisle during my early childhood years was, believe it or not, a FIRE! Carlisle did not have a lot of fires, but when we had one, it really got our undivided attention!

When the fire siren blew, everybody dropped whatever they were doing, and ran into their front yard. There, our friends and neighbors would share any information they knew about the whereabouts of the fire, and how severe it was. I believe it was Glen Milburn, who lived across the street, who eventually got a police scanner. That gave us the inside story on the fire, and of course catapulted us to one of the most reliable resources for fire information. Thanks, Glen.

Our home was located at 650 School Street, the main east-west road through Carlisle, so we had a good chance of seeing the fire truck fly by our house on the way to the fire.

Early on, the fire truck would be followed by a long line of cars driven by Carlisle citizens who had heard that this fire was "a good one" and would be worth their while to attend. Later on, the practice of following the fire truck was outlawed because of the accidents it created.

There are two distinct things that I remember about our small town fires. One was the night there was a gas station fire in Avon Lake, a small town about three miles northwest of Carlisle. That fire apparently caught my dad's attention, because our whole family piled into our 1950 Mercury, and away we flew down the gravel road to Avon Lake.

We were not disappointed. The fire was huge, and while we were watching the station burn, one of the gas pumps blew up! I remember the loud explosion and everyone running as fast as we could with our hands covering our heads! It was neat!

The other memory I have of Carlisle fires is that of actually meeting the firemen several times as they were called to a fire - at our home. We had a homemade outdoor brick fireplace where we burned the trash. In those days, everyone had a "burn barrel" or something similar, and there were no city burning laws.

I loved the job of burning the trash, especially when I knew there were plastic containers or plastic bags in the trash. I had discovered that these items, when lit, had the ability to drop "fire bombs" from the air as you waved them back and forth.

Unfortunately, these firebombs could be unruly and on more than one occasion, caught the dry grass next to the fireplace on fire! And that set the pasture area next to it on fire too. On the bright side, I got to meet the firemen as they came to put out the fire I had started, and it gave them a chance to tell my folks how much I had grown since the last time they were at our house.

As a little boy, I never once considered the destruction fires cause or the possibility that someone could be injured. The fire siren simply brought all activities to an instant halt, and for a few minutes we were totally absorbed with the excitement of the moment, which was far more exciting than the regular things that happened to us on a regular day in Carlisle.

The Three Darling Garnett Children
Jimmy, Patty, Howard

Chapter Two

Roller Derby

When I was around nine or ten years old, my older brother Howard, and older sister, Pat, and I started watching a popular weekly television program called Roller Derby.

It was an exciting game, consisting of both men and women teams, who would roller skate around a banked, oval track for points. The object of the game was for certain team members to skate around the track, catch the opposing team players, and pass them for points.

There were all sorts of maneuvers the players used - body blocks, trips, pushes, whip-around's, and occasionally someone would be thrown over the waist-high railing that surrounded the track. We suspected some of it might be fake, like on Saturday Night Wrestling (pronounced "raslin" back then), but it was still exciting to watch.

We each had our favorite team chosen from such illustrious groups as the Bay Area Bombers, Chicago Hawks, Texas Outlaws, Detroit Devils, and Los Angels T-Birds.

After watching the show several weeks, we begged our parents to buy us roller skates, and they did. These were not "shoe skates," but skates that clamped onto your street shoes and were tightened with a skate key.

The sidewalks near our house were not real smooth, but we found a perfect place to skate just a block away at the elementary school building. On one corner of the building, the flat roof extended out over a 20' wide walkway where the concrete was exceptionally smooth.

This provided an "L-shaped" Roller Derby track consisting of two 20' x 70' concrete slabs. The last slab was divided by a set of stairs in the middle. And, oh yes, there was a 10" metal grate that ran across the first section. I think its purpose was for water drainage, but to us it just presented a challenge. The slits in the grate were just a little wider than your skate wheel. Sometimes you could skate over the grate, while at other times it caught your wheel and stopped you dead in your tracks! You never knew how the grate was going to treat you on any given day.

You should have seen our Roller Derby games - there were blocks, trips, pushes, whip-arounds, and occasionally someone would be thrown over the waist-high concrete flower planters that bordered the walkway!

And once in a great while, there would be a "stair-jump." This was a move we perfected that would allow a skater to pass his opponent going airborne from the top of the stairs to the bottom of the stairs without ever touching even one stair!

I look back at those roller derby days and marvel how we kept from sustaining some really serious injuries. All the falls, jumps, and trips were on concrete, and the grate that caught your skate wheel would at least break your ankle if not totally tear your leg off at the hip!

The only plausible explanation is that the Garnett children's guardian angels were cushioning our falls! Those angels had practice protecting us from the Roller Derby antics, by protecting us previously from the pile-drivers, headlocks, arm bars, and body slams we executed in our front yard as a result of watching Saturday Night Wrestling (Raslin').

Chapter Three

Hitching A Ride From Dad

Me Age 3

One of the fondest memories I have of growing up in Carlisle took place when I was no more than four or five years old. It has to do with hitching a ride from my dad. If you looked west from our house, you could almost see the intersection of School Street and Highway 5 that went to Des Moines.

I knew in the late afternoon, my dad would be turning onto School Street from the highway as he journeyed home from his day of work at Des Moines Drug. I would ask my mom to tell me when it was about time for him to be coming home, so I could run up the sidewalk past two houses, and lean against the big tree in Stansberry's yard. As my dad drove by, he would see me waiting for him and would pull over to the curb so I could get into his car and "hitch a ride" home with him.

Thinking back, I can't imagine that car ride could have taken over a minute, but it seemed much longer to a little boy. In fact, it gave me plenty of time to do what needed to be done.

You see, my dad would set his lunchbox on the passenger seat, and when I got into the car, he placed the lunchbox on my lap. That worked out perfectly! No sooner would he pull away from the curb than I would flip open his lunch box to find an Oreo cookie, a Twinkie, a Hostess cupcake, or my favorite – half of a roast beef sandwich with ketchup!

I am not sure how I did it, but I managed to consume whatever "treasure" I found during that one-minute drive, and wipe my mouth off before I walked into the house.

I am sure my mom must have thought Dad was a "good eater' because his lunchbox was usually empty when he set it on the kitchen counter.

Dad 1955

I am also sure that my dad must have figured out my devious plan to intercept his leftovers, but, even so, he still seemed genuinely happy to see me and give me a ride home!

Chapter Four

The "Smokehouse"

Our garage was a one-car detached garage whose doors swung out horizontally. You opened these one door at a time. The garage stood a good 50 feet from the house. I suppose some people back then had attached garages, but the idea was something I never knew existed until years later. Dad did not always park in the garage, so it didn't make much difference if it was attached or not.

Between our garage and our house stood a much smaller building about one-third the size of the garage. This building was called the "smokehouse." Its name never portrayed its purpose.

My mom was originally from Virginia, and that is where I suspect the "smokehouse" got its name. A century earlier, before the days of refrigeration, a smokehouse was a small-enclosed shelter where families in the South would smoke their meat. It was a place where a fire could be kept smoldering for weeks, slowly releasing its smoke, and smoking the meat to preserve it. Then the smoked meat would hang in the smokehouse, safe from vermin and thieves.

As far as I know, no one ever smoked anything in our smokehouse - meat, cigarettes, or anything else. Our smokehouse was mainly used to store my mom's canning jars. She had hundreds of canning jars that lined the shelves that went around the room.

I did not go into the smokehouse much because along with the canning jars were spiders. They hid in the dark corners and would jump out at you and bite you and you might die. At least that is what my older brother and sister told me.

I have fond memories of our smokehouse because of its door. Yes, its door. You see, one could open the smokehouse door about an inch, and it would stay in that position. This created a very narrow "crack" if you stood 50 feet away. I did stand 50 feet away holding my Daisy Red Ryder, Daisy, BB gun rifle. I got it for my 9th birthday. My Red Ryder was like the one in the picture. It had a lever-cocking handle and couldhold well over a hundred BB's.

I got to be quite a good shot with my BB gun, eventually being able to shoot flies off the back garage wall at 20', and bumble bees off Mom's gladiolas at 30'. I also shot a few birds, and no, I did not have a guilty conscience like Opie,

Sheriff Taylor's son (you would have to see that episode).

What I also could do with that BB gun was to shoot through the "crack" by the smokehouse door from a good 50 feet away. And why on earth would I want to do that? Well, it had something to do with a little boy loving to hear the sound of breaking glass.

You see, with each shot through the door I could hear those canning jars breaking – it was simply music to my ears. The best part, of course, was when the next time my mom went into the smokehouse to get some jars, and I would hear her say, "We need to get that door fixed, Lyle! That stupid cat got in here again and broke some more of my jars!"

That stupid cat! I did not care for it much anyway, and he was the perfect scapegoat that allowed me to hone my shooting expertise, hear the sound of breaking glass, and get *him* in trouble with my mom. What could be more perfect?

Mom
Circa 1943

Chapter Five

Jessie's Drugstore

Jessie Bartholomew owned and operated a small drugstore at the east end of the downtown strip of shops in Carlisle. I liked to visit Jessie's as a little boy. It gained a place in my heart and in my memories because of two distinct things: the soda fountain and the jewelry counter.

In the mid-50's it was very common for drugstores to have a soda fountain where you could order soda pop and/or ice cream, and Jessie's was fortunate enough to have one of those.

I remember Jessie as a short little lady, not quite 5 foot tall I would guess. She was a nice lady, and always took time to be nice to the kids who came into her store.

If Mom was not in a big hurry, we could sit up on the counter stools and order a soda pop. We knew that spinning round-and-round on the stool would quickly bring unwanted correction from our mom or from Jessie, so we held that

An Old Time Soda Fountain
Similar To The One In Jessie's

activity to a minimum.

For a nickel we could order a regular fountain soda, but for a penny more, you could turn that soda into a flavored taste delight. My favorites came down to a selection of three drinks: cherry coke, chocolate coke, or a "green river," which was advertised as *"a lime soda drink with just a touch of lemon."* Actually, it was not so much the taste that attracted me to this drink, but the way you could look through your drinking glass and see everything in a pretty emerald hue.

Usually, I ordered a chocolate coke because almost anything with chocolate on it or in it earned its way to the top of my taste list. I distinctly remember one time that Jessie gave me both a "shot" of cherry and a "shot" of chocolate for six cents! She winked at me and made me feel like what she had done was a secret just between her and me. I liked her even more after we had that "secret" between us.

It was just plain neat to sit up to the counter and sip on your soda. It made you feel like the world was ok. All the pressures and stresses of a seven-year-old would just vanish away at Jessie's soda fountain.

The other memory I have of Jessie's has to do with the jewelry she sold. It was some of the prettiest and "most glittery" jewelry that a second grade boy had ever seen! It was not until many years later that I discovered the brilliant bright lights shining on the jewelry is what made it was so pretty. Some of those nickel rings lost their luster when you took them out of the case.

Not sure why but at that young age I seemed to have a problem keeping a girlfriend. In fact, I would say I averaged a couple of girlfriends a month!

I would like to tell you that it was I who ended the relationships, but I think it was most likely the girl. We called it "getting dumped," and I was no stranger to that sad experience.

Age 5

Back to the jewelry. I would purchase a pretty ring for my girlfriend for 5 cents. These were really neat rings because they were adjustable. You could squeeze the ring band and make it smaller, or pull on it and it would fit the larger finger. I never had to know the size of my girlfriend's ring finger – all the rings fit all the girls.

By my third or fourth month in the second grade, I was making so many trips to Jessie's to buy rings, I started buying five or six rings at a time. This was much more convenient for me since I had no transportation, and it allowed me to frequently take out my ring collection and view each ring in the sunlight. I now wonder why I never bargained with Jessie for a volume discount. I also wonder why I never asked for my rings back when I got dumped. I am absolutely positive that my girlfriends tossed them in the trash anyway. Girls are funny that way! That could have saved me a lot of nickels!

Jessie's Drugstore - where the thirst of a little boy got quenched at her fountain, and his hurting heart got mended by buying another ring.

Chapter Six

Jarvey's

There was one place that I was always eager to go with my mom or dad, and that place was "Jarvey's." I never thought much about the fact that Jarvey's was a grocery store, only that there was a man there by the name of Jarvey who was nice to me, and he gave the kids candy.

Jarvey's was owned by Jarvey and Sybil Owens, a couple who must have been in their 60's – or at least they seemed that old to me. I remember Jarvey as a round-faced guy with red checks who was always smiling. He seemed to like kids. When my folks were ready to "ring up" their groceries at the counter, I would always make certain I was easy to be seen. That's when and where we would get the candy.

From behind the counter Jarvey would pull out what looked like a roll of adding machine paper. On this roll of paper were stuck little colored, candy dots. He called these "Jarvey pills" and said they "were good for whatever ailed you." This treat motivated me to "stay good" while my folks were shopping for their grocery items, and also made Jarvey a friend to every kid who came in his store.

Each year when pictures were taken at the school, there was a candy bar waiting for each child who brought Jarvey a picture to stick on his big poster board that hung on the wall.

There are a couple of other things I remember about Jarvey's. Every Saturday morning at 10:00AM, Jarvey would host a drawing from among all the cash register receipts of that week. These had been signed on the back, and the winner of the drawing received a $25 gift certificate for groceries.

I never remember my folks winning the drawing, but I do remember standing in the crowd of 40-50 people while Jarvey read the name of the winner from the steps of his store.

I also recall accompanying my mom or dad to the back of the store where the meat counter stretched along the width of the store. You could feel the cold on the thick glass windows, and when no one was looking, you could touch your tongue on it (not particularly a sanitary practice!)

But the main attraction at the meat counter was the two men who apparently were the butchers, Bill and Homer. Homer almost always had a cigarette dangling from his mouth (it was the 50's remember), and I would watch that cigarette very closely.

You see, my brother and sister had told me that the ashes from Homer's cigarette would often fall into the hamburger, and I wanted to see that happen! Unfortunately, I never did, and now I wonder if the whole story was made up for my benefit.

There was one other attraction for me at Jarvey's. It was on the floor of the last aisle pushed under the tall shelving. I had no idea what it was, but it was a flat, round metal container about 30" across.

The top of the container would spin while the base of the container stayed stationary. I would quickly make my way through the store, get on my hands and knees, pull out this spinning thing, sit on it, and spin round-and-round! I have learned only recently, that it was some sort of a container that held sewing machine needles and parts. But of course, I did not need to know what it was to know it was fun to sit on it and spin around!

All this, and more, awaiting you at Jarvey's!

Jim Justis, Jarvey & Sybil Owens, Bill Hines, Homer Patterson
The school pictures just above Homer's head are from kids
who received a candy bar for their picture.

Chapter Seven

Sounds From Sixth Street

As I mentioned earlier in the Introduction, I visualize my memories as being stored in little boxes of my brain. The "combination" that opens the memorybox can be a sight, a sound, a touch, a taste, a smell.

The memory box about Sixth Street is unlocked by sounds: a distant train or a mourning dove.

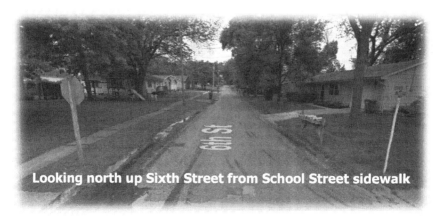

Looking north up Sixth Street from School Street sidewalk

A distant train. Sixth Street intersected School Street from the north just two houses east of our house. At age six, I had never actually walked up Sixth Street because I was not allowed to cross the street.

But as I walked to kindergarten, I would often stand on the sidewalk, looking up Sixth Street, trying to catch a glimpse of a distant train I could hear. It had such a soothing sound, an enchanting sound, a mesmerizing sound. It was a sound that stirred the imaginations of a little six-year-old boy.

If I shut my eyes, I could envision the train as it rolled down the tracks. Sometimes it carried passengers, sometimes it carried coal, sometimes it carried cars, but almost always it carried hobos.

Today, nearly 60 years later, the sound of a far away train will instantly transport me back to that sidewalk across from Sixth Street in Carlisle. The sound of a distant train instantly "unlocks" the little box that holds all those memories, and I am a little six year-old-boy again, filled with wonder.

I must have been in my forties, while visiting my folks in Carlisle, when I decided to drive up Sixth Street and see just where that train crossed the road. Although I had lived in Carlisle until I was 18, I never remember seeing just where that train went.

To my amazement and disappointment, **I found no train tracks. I came to the realization that day that there was never a train up that street!** The only train tracks in Carlisle were a mile east of our house near the downtown area. Somehow the sound of those passing trains must have echoed to the unseen end of Sixth Street. I, frankly, found this hard to believe but could see no other alternative. There was no train –

ever – down that street! The sound was deceptive – I would have sworn the train was just out of sight!

I finally concluded that I would not allow the soothing "click-a-tee-clack, click-a-tee-clack" memory of the distant train to be diminished by the fact that Sixth Street was not the source of its origin. It didn't matter. The train was somewhere, carrying its passengers, or its coal, or its cars, and its hobos.

A mourning dove. The sound of a mourning dove also unlocks this memory box for me. My folks called these birds "rain crows" – I guess because they thought they "sang" before it rained? They are also called Turtle Doves.

I hate to confess this, but I thought for years they were "*morning* doves" because they sang in the *morning* instead of the *evening*. (Stop laughing!)

I had no idea what these birds actually looked like, only what they sounded like. The mourning dove gets its name from its low, mournful call. It is a very eerie, mournful sound – thus, "*mourning*" dove.

Like the sound of the train, I thought the sound of the mourning dove was coming from somewhere just out of sight up Sixth Street. When I heard their mournful calls, I would stop and look up the street to catch a glimpse of one of them – but I never did.

The sound of a passing train and the mournful call of a dove. These were two sounds that fascinated a little 6-year-old boy on his way to Kindergarten. If the truth be told, to this day they still fascinate a 64-year-old man. They are "the sounds from Sixth Street" in Carlisle.

Chapter Eight

The Carlisle Movie Theater

We just called it "the movie house." It was located in downtown Carlisle, about a block north of School and 1st Streets. In fact, almost everything was within a block of the intersection of School Street and 1st Street, because downtown Carlisle was only a block long.

Present-day building which housed the Carlisle Movie Theater in the 50' & 60's.

The Carlisle movie theater has some warm memories for me. When I was 4-5 years old, there would be a free movie matinee for kids on a Saturday afternoon just prior to Christmas, and afterward Santa would appear at the corner with bags of candy for everyone. This is my earliest memory of going to the Carlisle movie theater.

When I was eight years old, I attended the Sci-Fi movie called "The Blob" at the Carlisle movie house. This movie featured Steve McQueen and was directed by a man who would later become a Carlisle resident and a good friend of mine, Russell Doughten, Jr. In 1972, Russ produced the Christian blockbuster movie "A Thief In The Night"(which boasts a 300 million world-wide viewing audience) and starred two Carlisle young people, Mike and Coleen Niday.

"The Blob" had a really scary part in which this out-of-control, mass of gelatin thing was loose in a movie theater. I remember how I pulled my feet up under my legs and sat on them (just in case that blob thing was in the movie house!). The seats were made out of wood with no padding, and this proved to be quite uncomfortable, but I wasn't going to let that gooey blob stuff get me!

I also remember the concession window. The line to order popcorn and a drink was always long unless you ducked out of the movie a few seconds ahead of the intermission.

It was at this very concession window that I first became acquainted with a new product that had just hit the market - barbeque potato chips. The theater was giving them a "test run" on their patrons. One of us bought a bag, tried them and passed the bag around. Then, everyone bought a bag and they sold out of barbeque chips that Saturday night. They were new, they were different, and we felt we were lucky to have them!

The Carlisle movie house has yet another memory for me. This memory occurred in the rear of the theater on the right side in the two seats next to the wall. Yes, you guessed it – that's where I received my first kiss. I must have been in sixth grade, and frankly was not practiced at such things. I must not have done too well because there was only one kiss. Either it overwhelmed her completely, or she didn't care for another. And yes, I remember the girl's name, but I see no reason to tell you who she was. You might tell her parents, or worse yet, she could just deny it ever happened.

My last memory of the theater occurred when I was sixteen. This was the very last time I attended the Carlisle theater. My friends and I went to the movie that Saturday night "armed" with our newest purchases – small plastic pistols that shot "beans." We called them "bean guns," and had purchased them at the Atlantic Mills store on 2nd and Euclid in Des Moines.

We bought our tickets and entered with our bean guns stuck in our jacket pockets out of sight (can you imagine doing something like that and getting caught today?). Once inside, we ascended the stairs to the balcony so we would have a good view of the people sitting in their seats. That was my first time in the balcony because the balcony was always a lot warmer than the main floor due to no air conditioning. But since we did not have air conditioning in any of our houses or cars, we didn't miss it!

There were very few people in the balcony that night, and when we entered, the couple that was there left. Not sure why? To our amazement and delight, we discovered that the theater ceiling was made out of tin – one large square after another of tin tiles. I am sure the ceiling was a beautiful sight with the lights on, but since this was a movie theater, the lights were off most of the time and no one noticed the ceiling. This tin ceiling was the type of tin that made a loud "plink" noise when struck by a bean.

We waited until the movie was fully underway, then each of us took a shot at that tin ceiling! You could hear the beans "plink" the ceiling, then fall into the lower section where people were sitting.

That night we realized how important it was to have paid attention in geometry class, because with very little effort, we could calculate where the bean would drop. It was extremely funny watching the person get hit by a falling bean and swat at it as though it were an attacking insect. And of course, with each shot, all of us would scrunch down in our seats so the people below could not see us up in the balcony.

It really was great fun, although it did not last a real long time. After each of us had taken a couple of shots, the theater manage ascended the stairs into the balcony and told us we would need to cut our movie going short that night. I guess since we were the only people in the balcony, it did not require a detective to figure out who the "plinking" culprits were.

We did not get to see the last of the movie, but then we had not seen the first of the movie either because we were shooting beans, so it was not a big loss.

I can still hear those beans as they ricocheted off the tin ceiling - plink…plink…plink. I have to admit, it was by far the highlight of my movie going career. In fact, if the truth were known, I would most likely do it all over again if I could just find that bean gun!

Chapter Nine

The Fourth Of July

Of all my childhood memories of Carlisle, the Carlisle 4th of July celebration holds more memories than any other single event.

Normally, the celebration lasted for two days, usually part of the 3rd and then all of the 4th. The city fathers would contract with a traveling carnival to set up at the Carlisle city park and serve as the centerpiece of the activities. We were excited to go to the park, but we needed to exercise caution because the people who ran the carnival were gypsies and they would steal you away if you got too close to them or wore bright colored clothing.

The park was and is located on the northeast side of town. If you pass by the park on First Street , you will be on your way to Avon Lake, a small town about three miles north west of Carlisle (and yes, it does actually have a lake – in fact it has two lakes).

The park entrance, at that time, was on the southwest corner of the park property. I remember two brick columns that you drove between to enter, and once inside, the road made a big loop and brought you back to where you had started.

The best way I know to share those memories I have of the 4th of July is to break them down into "categories."

The Parade. The parade signaled the official start of the celebration. Before I was old enough to ride on a baseball team float or march in the band, I sat on the curb in front of our house at 650 School Street eagerly waiting to run into the street to pick up candy that was tossed from the floats. A boy could actually bring in quite a haul of goodies from the parade if he were fast on his feet.

The parade started in downtown Carlisle by the grain elevator, went west up School Street by our house, turned north up 5th, then east on Market Street, then north on 1st Street, and ended up at the park entrance. One year, after the parade had passed by our house, we drove to my grandma's house that was only a block away from the park. That day I got to see the parade twice, but better than that, I got to pick up candy twice! I took in a really good haul that year!

The parade was a typical small town parade with a fire truck (singular), ambulance, high school marching band, a few business floats, The Old Dudley Band playing bluegrass from a flatbed truck, a couple of church floats, a couple of veteran groups, some horses (behind which you never wanted to march), and some Shriner guys riding little go carts. I always asked my folks to buy me one of those, but they never did.

One of the most unusual "floats" we ever had in the parade was Denny Van Ryswyk driving his 18-wheeler *backwards* for the entire parade route! I believe he had just won some kind of driving award and was asked to illustrate his expertise. When you stop to think about the skill required to back an 18-wheeler through a parade, it was quite impressive. Plus, I am guessing that feat has never been duplicated and should most likely appear in the Guinness Book of World Records.

Lunch At Grandma's. Since Grandma and Grandpa's house was only a block away from the park, it was always convenient to go to their house for lunch on the 4th. My mom would prepare fried chicken and potato salad, and might I add that absolutely no one makes either any better! As good as it was, I was so excited to get to the park where all the action was, I gulped down my food and pestered my parents to hurry up. They liked going to the park to hear the afternoon concerts. In later years, I was able to leave for the park before my parents did, but only after getting strict instructions about what I was and was not to do. I was also cautioned about the gypsies who ran the carnival.

The Carnival. On that short walk to the park, my mind was just in a whirl! My little legs were walking as fast as they could while I was thinking about the cotton candy, the games of chance, the ice cream bars, the prizes, the smell of the midway, and most of all *"the mechanical crane drop"* (the forerunner of the stuffed animal crane machines we see in restaurant lobbies today).

The prizes were things like shiny rings, beautiful necklaces, colored pins, and a couple of watches that were buried where only a highly skilled mechanical-crane-drop-operator could reach them!

To become that skilled, one would need to practice for at least 10 sessions. Of course, each new play window had its own mechanical crane machine with its own unique characteristics, so the strategy you used on one crane was no good on a different crane.

I went directly to the MCD (mechanical crane drop) area and studied how the players were playing before I starting plotting my strategy.

I remember winning a ring once. It wasn't even made of metal – it was plastic! The bright light above those prizes made them look much more expensive and shiny than they actually were!

One of my most vivid memories of being at the park on the 4th was the day that my good friend, Scotty James (now of James Oil Company fame) found a $20 bill on the park grounds. I was so envious of Scotty as I watched him go from person to person showing them the $20 bill and saying, "I'm rich, I'm plumb rich!" And in those days, he actually was plumb rich with that $20 bill. I will have to ask him when I see him next, if he remembers what he spent all that money for.

Motorcycle Hill. Our trip to the Carlisle park for the 4th, had to include a brief visit to "motorcycle hill," which was located almost out of sight on the north side of the park. You needed

to know about where the gap was between the trees to find the trail made by the motorcycles. It was easy to miss. As you peered over the edge, the tracks disappeared straight down until they reached a flat area near the North River.

Motorcycle hill was just that – a hill that motorcycles climbed. It was no more than 100 feet long, but as you neared the top, it actually seemed to go straight up at a 90-degree angle! I remember one time the three of us kids tried to run up motorcycle hill, but we could not reach the very top. I never saw any motorcycles actually climb the hill either, but the ruts that were visible served as evidence that someone was accomplishing that feat.

It must have been so cool in the mid-50's to watch those guys with their duck tailed greasy hair and cuffed blue jeans, their pack of cigarettes rolled up in the sleeve of their

white T- shirts, gather at the bottom of the hill with their "James Dean Harleys" to make a run up the hill.

I wonder now how many of these young men flipped their bikes over their heads at the top of the hill because they did not get up enough speed to make it all the way up. It would have been a terrifying thing to attempt, only a little better than the humility of being dared to try it and backing out!

Yes sir, every 4th I made my annual journey to see motorcycle hill at the park. I am sure you would have been impressed too, if you were a young boy in the 50's.

Fireworks. If someone said "fireworks" in those days, we would not think about "a fireworks show" that you watched in the sky. To us, "fireworks" meant those really neat little "sticks of dynamite" that you could throw and watch them explode!

Our family would make an annual pilgrimage to Lineville, MO, just across the Iowa state line, because fireworks were legal to buy in Missouri. We would save up for months anticipating the trip to purchase our "stash" of firecrackers for the 4th.

I was never interested in fireworks that were pretty. I wanted the ones that made the most noise and could blow the can the highest up in the air. The best ones to buy were cherry bombs, 2 inch-ers, and M-80's. I think all of these are outlawed now.

But back then, there were a lot of things one could do with fireworks like these three. You could set them under a can and blow it 15 feet into the air, or you could drop them in a big empty barrel, and the sound from the explosion was magnified times over!

Throwing them in a farm pond was neat too, because they were waterproof and would explode under water. Some times you could see a small fish or frog float to the top that had been too near the explosion and lost their life. I remember the time that our excitement was at an all-time fever pitch when my brother, Howard, tried to throw a cherry bomb out of our bedroom window. What made it so exciting was the fact that when he threw it, it hit the window frame and bounced back into our bedroom. I wish I could remember whether or not it blew up in our room, it surely had to! But I do remember clearly our dad threatening to take our whole stash away for such an irresponsible deed.

We did buy some Roman candles one year because they were "not as dangerous." These fireworks are a 12-inch long rod (candle) and shoot a fireball out one end. Unfortunately, they do become "dangerous" when dropped after lighting them.

Yep, after lighting it I dropped it, and everyone in the backyard took cover! It would shoot off its fireball, then spin around like a top! We never knew when it was going to shoot the next fireball or in whose direction! I remember all of us hiding behind some solid object so we wouldn't get hit! Our parents had warned us about the danger of firecrackers "shooting your eye out" (this phrase was also used for BB guns) and we did not want that to happen. It seems pretty funny now, but at the time, I do not remember anyone laughing.

I'd have to say one of the very best times we ever had shooting fireworks was the evening that Dad's men's softball team gathered at our house for one of their frequent get-togethers. Once those men got wind of the fact that we had a big stash of firecrackers that were "the good ones," they eagerly joined us in blowing up as much stuff as we could find. At the time I was amazed that those grown men had as much fun shooting off fireworks as we did. But from my present perspective of 60 years plus, I can see how I would enjoy it almost as much as I did back then, except you can't buy those "good ones" any more. Today's fireworks are the "sissy kind."

Chapter Ten

A Garnett Christmas

I like to watch the annual showing of the TV movie "A Christmas Story" because it so aptly reveals how life was in the 1950's (except for the "leg lamp" that sat in the front window – you would have to have seen the movie to understand!).

As I think about the Christmas seasons the Garnett family observed, several things come to mind.

The Tree. The first thing I think of was our Christmas tree. It was always a live tree, because I do not think artificial trees were "invented" yet, at least no one we knew had one. Our tree was never a big one, but that did not seem to make any difference. It was always beautiful. We often would buy it at the Christmas tree lot in downtown Carlisle.

Dad Sitting In Front Of Our Tree
(Obviously A Bad Year For Christmas Trees!)

We would help Dad decorate the tree. It was neat seeing the ornaments each year, which we so delicately hung on the branches. Our lights were wired in "series," meaning if one light was burned out, the whole string would not work.

Dad would then have to go down the light string, testing the lights one by one to see which one(s) were burned out and replace them. We always wondered how you could put away a strand of good lights in January and some of them burned out when you plugged them in the next Christmas. Why would a light bulb burn out if it were not being used? Oh, the mysteries of Christmas.

The lights in the 1950's seemed bigger and brighter than the lights we have today, at least through the eyes of a little boy. Their warm glow was so inviting as they proclaimed, "Christmas is here!"

My favorite lights were the ones that bubbled once they warmed up. I remember that us kids would sit expectantly, waiting for those "bubble lights" to start doing their thing, and when they did, we were mesmerized by them.

As a Dad, I thought it would be neat to reproduce that memory for my children, so I bought a strand of the bubble lights and added them to my tree. Not only were they pricey, but I had the hardest time getting them to work. In fact, after replacing them twice, I just gave up! Could it be that the ones in the 1950's worked better than the ones I bought forty years later?

After the ornaments and the lights came the garland. That was reserved for my older brother or sister or one of my parents, because my arms were too short to hang it on the tree. I saw trees in the stores where the garland resembled rolling waves in the ocean as it went up and down in such a meticulous pattern. Our garland looked like it had been hung by a blind man coming off a two-week binge.

The finishing touch on the tree was the tinsel (those little strands of silver). We were anxious to get the tinsel on the tree so we would grab a handful and throw it on, but we would soon be told to lay them on the tree just a few at a time. I remember telling my own kids the same thing when we decorated our tree because they had the same tendency to throw it on in clumps like I did.

When I was a little, the Christmas tree was a magical thing! Sometimes we would turn out the lights in the room and just sit and look at the tree. Everything just glowed! That was a very integral part of Christmas for me.

The Gifts. Before Christmas, we would receive a box of gifts in the mail from our relatives in North Carolina. We were always told "they meant well," but they were not so good at picking out gifts. One year I even got a bottle of liquid deodorant! I did not have any hair under my arms yet, but I am sure that if I had, that stuff would have burned it all off. It smelled terrible and burned your eyes!

I am not sure why in this picture my brother and I are holding Christmas gifts but my sister is holding nothing. The obvious answer would be that she had not been "good" during the year and was now suffering the dreaded consequences at Christmas!

I remember the Christmas that each of us kids received a brand new Kodak "Brownie" camera. These cameras were very simple to use and even came with a couple of rolls of film. So, the next day, we donned our winter apparel and went outside to take pictures.

But these were film cameras, not digital cameras, so you could not see the pictures you were taking until you had them developed at the drugstore, and that normally took 7-10 days!

But we were in a hurry to see the pictures we were taking, so to move things along, we took pictures rather rapidly. In fact, it only took us about 7 minutes to go through our two rolls of film each! You might wonder how we found so many interesting things to take pictures of outside our house in the winter? That was a problem.

When our pictures came back, we noticed that each of us had taken pictures of the same things, just with three different cameras. For instance there were three pictures each of such interesting things like "kitty in the tree," "kitty on the ground," "Jimmy by the tree," "Patty by the tree," "Howard by the tree," "Patty in the tree," "Jimmy in the tree," and "Jimmy with BB gun by the tree and the kitty"

You get the picture (no pun intended)? It was the biggest waste of film ever known to mankind! But we learned from our impatience, and the next time we shot pictures, it took us a whole 15 minutes to take the whole roll! Unfortunately, they were still boring! Later on, when we grew tired of taking pictures (and paying to have them developed) we would find pictures from two different Christmas's on one roll of film! In other words, that was the only time we took any pictures!

The Baptist Church Program. I also remember attending the Christmas program at the Baptist Church each year. The church would be packed with people who showed up to watch their kids and grandkids. My reason for wanting to go was a bit more food oriented – they gave away a big brown bag of candy to all the kids! If you were lucky, you would get a bag that had numerous pieces of those chocolate covered candies with vanilla crème inside. The hard candy was good too, but nothing was better than something with chocolate on it. A "bad bag" of candy was one where you got more than one piece of fruit! That fruit took up a lot of room in the bag where good candy could have gone.

One year, my dad wore his bathrobe to the Christmas program! He was asked to play the part of one of the wise men, and sing "We Three Kings" in a men's trio. After hearing Dad practice at home, I went around the house singing, "We three king-sa-orian-r." I had no idea what that meant, but I sure liked the tune.

You know how it is when you are not real sure about the words – you sort of slur all the words together to just get through the phrase. I guess it sounded close enough to the right words, that no one ever corrected me. It wasn't till years later that I finally realized the words were "We three kings of Orient are." Now that makes sense! The other didn't.

Did I ever get the words to other songs wrong? I found out that Elvis's song actually said "Return *to Sender*" instead of "Return *December*," and Johnny Horton's song was "North to Alaska, goin' north, *the rush is on*" instead of "North to Alaska, goin' north, to *Russia's zone*." I am sure there are others too numerous to mention.

The Tour of the Lights. Every Christmas season our family would take one evening to drive around looking at the Christmas lights. Apparently, our 1950 Mercury did not have a good defrosting system, because I remember constantly having to use my coat sleeve to "clear the fog off the window" so I could see out.

We would first tour the town of Carlisle. Christmas lighting was not like today where every other house is decorated. There were only a few sections in Carlisle where houses had lights, and they were not as extreme as today. Mostly, those who had lights on their houses lived in the newer sections of Carlisle, and were probably used to lighting their houses in the areas where they were from. When one house got lights, it served to be the inspiration for neighbors to light theirs. There were also decorations on the light poles in downtown Carlisle, but most of them did not light up.

Then after touring Carlisle, we would drive to Des Moines and tour down town Des Moines first. Not only was it decorated along both sides of the town streets, but also some of the storefront windows displayed Christmas scenes.

Walnut Street
At Christmas
Downtown
Des Moines
1950's

I believe it was Younkers that had fascinating window displays that were always worth seeing, especially because they had moveable figures in those displays.

From downtown Des Moines, we would head home to Carlisle by way of Fleur Drive. There we were always blown away at the fabulous lighting on those homes. One of those homes was owned by Orville Lowe, a car dealer (now called Stivers), and was always the best of the homes on Fleur Drive. He incorporated the newer style lighting scheme that used just one color to trim the whole house - blue, red, green, or white. It was a drastic change from the usual multicolored light design, but it really caught your eye.

The lights in the 1950's seemed to be much different than the ones today. They seemed bigger and brighter, and much more colorful, and at times, if they were covered with a layer of snow, they had a beautiful glow. Or, at least that is how it seemed through the eyes of a little boy from Carlisle at Christmas.

In my early days, riding around to see the Christmas lights was a highlight of the Christmas season. It cost nothing, was something we only did once a year, and seemed to set the mood for the beautiful transformation the world takes on at Christmas time.

Santa Bites The Dust. I remember the year we discovered that Santa did not exist. In my early years, our routine on Christmas Eve was to go to my grandma's house and eat supper ("supper" was the term we used to describe the evening meal as opposed to lunch or dinner which was the mid-day meal). After supper we all would anxiously pile in the car and head back to our house to open Christmas presents. There were a few presents under the tree before we went to Grandma's, but there were a lot more upon returning home after supper.

Just as we would climb into the car, we would hear sleigh bells, and Grandpa Fred would inform us that he had just seen Santa's sleigh in the sky. My brother Howard has these very sleigh bells that grandpa would ring each year because of the fond memories they hold for us.

This one Christmas Eve as we ended supper, we noticed that our dad had disappeared. While the dishes were being gathered, us three kids snuck into the bedroom and peered out the window that faced the garage. To our surprise there was our dad taking three brand new red sleds from Grandpa's garage and putting them in the trunk of our car! Later that evening we noticed the tags on the sled said "From Santa," but we knew who Santa really was.

So, the gig was up, and we knew Santa was Mom and Dad. We also noticed that night that Grandpa Fred had hidden sleigh bells under his coat. We didn't tell anyone what we had discovered, because everybody seemed to enjoy the "ruse", and we saw no reason to ruin it for them.

The new sleds went a long way toward softening the blow that Santa did not exist. Knowing the truth also supplied the answer to why "Santa" never gave us all toys, but had to mix clothes in the presents!

Carlisle Christmas memories are good memories of trees, pretty lights, glimmering tinsel, liquid deodorant, bags of candy, sleds, and Brownie cameras. Memories that make me smile as I close my eyes and remember.

Garnett Family Portrait About 1952

Chapter Eleven

Shooting Rats At The Dump

When I was ten or eleven years old, one activity that turned into a family outing was that of shooting rats at the Carlisle city dump. Yes, you read that correctly, shooting rats at the dump! I guess it should more accurately be called "shooting *at* rats at the dump," because we actually shot very few of them.

With today's focus on ecological concerns, it sounds almost unbelievable that there was a place, just outside of town, where open burning and open dumping were allowed. In fact, it was not only allowed, it was *encouraged*!

The Carlisle dump was east of Carlisle, across the railroad tracks, and down the gravel road about a mile, then to the left. Several acres had been set-aside for people to pull their pickups, cars, or trailers up to the edge of the garbage piles, and add theirs to the pile.

What was in the dump? There were old refrigerators

with their doors removed, brown paper bags full of who-knows-what (plastic grocery bags had not come on the scene yet), rusted bicycles, broken toys, worn out toasters, broken chairs, davenports, and just about every other item you could imagine that someone would no longer want or need.

There were several areas where trash was smoldering underneath piles of debris. I have to tell you, the smell that place was literally "breathtaking" - simply atrocious!

That reminds me of the day I came to the realization that the pretty red glow you could see from the SE 14th Street viaduct was the Des Moines dump smoldering. Its beauty at night faded once I knew what it was.

On to the rat shooting. My dad was in possession of my grandpa Fred's 1911, octagon-barrel, Remington, 12-shot, pump action, 22 caliber rifle. It was pretty heavy for a little boy to shoot, but I never wanted to mention that to anyone.

I do not know how the practice got started, but about once a month, the whole family would jump into the car and head down to the dump. Do you think we may have been starved for entertainment or what?

It might be an accurate recollection, or it might just be a memory seen through the eyes of a ten old boy, but those rats were huge! I remember some of them were as big as small cats!

I don't remember that I ever shot a rat myself. In fact, if my memory serves me right, my mom was the only family member that ever "bagged" one of those rats. I guess we were bad shots. And "No," we did NOT have it stuffed or mount its head on the wall.

Chapter Twelve

Sunday Afternoon Rides

It was not uncommon on a Sunday afternoon for me to be told, "Jimmy, get your shoes on - we're going for a ride!" (I am not sure why we needed to wear shoes to ride in the car, but we did.) That activity, going for a ride, was one that we three kids were accustomed to and enjoyed. It is a good childhood memory.

I found out as an adult, though, that the practice of "going for a ride" is not something everyone enjoyed as a child. For example, I remember saying to my wife, Ginny, shortly after we were married, "Hey, Honey, do you want to go for a ride?" Her reply was, "Go for a ride to where?" I found out then, that for many people "going for a ride" implies a destination and a specific route to get there. A leisurely ride in the car to just enjoy the trip is foreign to many people. But that is how I grew up – with Sunday afternoon rides. There was no destination and there was no route to get there. You went where you went, and you were there when you arrived.

Mom And Dad
Circa 1943

Dad always drove slowly, so we could have the back windows down. Since there were three of us kids, we would often fight over (I mean discuss) who "got the window seats." Sometimes, the loser would elect to sit in the front with Mom and Dad rather than sit in the middle in the back. After all, everybody knew "You couldn't see nothin' from the middle of the back seat!"

So, where did we go on our "rides?" Well, we first would start with our town of Carlisle, and slowly go up one street and down the other. My folks would comment on who had moved, and who had built, who had a baby, and who had need of painting their house or mowing their yard.

The cemetery was often the next stop on our Sunday afternoon ride, although we would not actually "stop." We would just drive through and glance at the names on the grave markers. As a little boy, it was a bit eerie for me to see the names on the graves of people who had just recently died. I had known these people when they were alive and walking around – now they were lying there beneath that mound of dirt. It was not a pleasant thing for a little boy to ponder, but a necessary exposure to real life (and death).

Often we would wind our way into the country, going ever so slowly so as to not stir up the dust on the gravel road. We would cross old rusted bridges, go by the ruins of the "haystack murders," or comment on how this one family's front yard looked very similar to the junk yard. It had rusty, turned over appliances, broken bicycles, abandoned toys, and piles of garbage.

I recall vividly the Sunday afternoon my dad saw a snake crossing the gravel road out east of Carlisle. He got so excited that he almost put the car in the ditch! He drove up and back, and up and back, till the snake had parts of him that were flatter than a pancake. Then Dad got out of the car and threw his knife at the snake . In case you couldn't tell, my dad did not like snakes (and he passed that dislike on to me).

Every kid who's ever gone for a ride on a Sunday afternoon knows that he must wait for just the right moment before popping the crucial question: "Can we get an ice cream cone?" Often my folks would say, "Yes," because Dad liked ice cream, especially butter-pecan (and so do I).

We would then end up at the Carlisle Dairy Queen, located at the corner of 5th Street and Highway 5, or if our afternoon ride had taken us closer to Des Moines, we would go to Reed's Ice Cream Shop just a couple of blocks from the State Fairgrounds. Reed's had a little boy figure on the roof eating a big ice cream cone that could be seen from blocks away. We always competed to see who would spot him first!

Sometimes we would eat our ice cream cone at the place we stopped, and other times eat it in the car on the way home. It really didn't matter. An ice cream cone was the perfect ending to "a Sunday afternoon ride."

It never occurred to me then, but looking back on those family Sunday afternoon rides, I realize now that they taught me something about life. They taught me the importance of not traveling the road so fast that the only focus is the destination, and not the ride itself. I think we call it today, "smelling the roses and enjoying the journey."

Howard, Pat, and Jim
1956

Chapter Thirteen

Summers In Carlisle

What did one do in Carlisle in the summer in the mid-50's? It was definitely different than today, in that there were very few organized activities for kids. Little League was over by early July, and then you were on your own.

We found plenty to do in the summer, and really did not complain much about being bored. It is funny though, that some of the activities that completely captivated our attention for a time, were abandoned as quickly as they were started. Let me share of few of those with you.

Cap Guns. One summer we got caught up in shooting cap guns. The caps came in a paper roll with about 100 caps per roll. The cap itself was a little raised bump that was filled with a very small explosive. The roll of caps wound its way inside a toy cap pistol. Pulling on the trigger would advance the roll just enough for the hammer to strike the cap and make a sound much like a gun shot. The used up cap roll came out the top of the gun by the hammer, and was to be torn off and thrown away when it became long.

You could buy a little box of five rolls of caps for a nickel, so there was a lot of "cap shooting enjoyment" with each nickel box containing almost 500 shots.

Not only did the caps sound like you were shooting a real gun, but there were two other "bonuses." One was the smell that the cap gave off when it fired (most likely the smell of gunpowder). If I close my eyes and concentrate for a minute, I can once again smell that sweet aroma. I never asked anyone else, but I assume other people liked the smell too? It would make me feel a bit odd to find out that I was the only one who liked it!

The second "bonus" was the fact that when the cap fired, smoke came out of the barrel of your pistol. It not only looked neat, but if you hurried, you could put your mouth over the barrel, suck in the smoke, and blow it out again! It was as though you were "smoking" like the adults.

I realize now, of course, that this practice was most likely not a healthy one for kids to engage in, but in those days there was no telling you it was bad for you to smoke – either tobacco or cap smoke.

I remember that this cap-shooting craze coincided with our relatives' from North Carolina coming to stay with us one summer. Our family had gone to visit my mother's mom, Grandma Horton, in Mount Airy (called Mayberry on the Andy Griffith show), North Carolina. For some reason, someone thought it would be a great idea if she and her three kids came back to Iowa with us for a few months.

Looking back, I do not know how any of us survived that trip home. There were five in our family and four in theirs. That made three adults and six kids less than twelve years of age in one car! Apparently, the details of that trip home were so painful, my mind has blotted them from my memory. My siblings and I fought enough already, and to add their bickering to ours, must have been somewhere short of a Heavenly delight!

Back to the cap shooting. For two whole months we would shoot cap guns every single day. You woke up in the morning planning your strategy as to how to outwit your fellow cap gunners. With our relatives living with us, and a few friends from the neighborhood, there were plenty of people to divide up into two or three teams.

If someone pointed their gun at you and shot, you were killed, or at least "winged," which would make you sit out of the game for a few minutes. As you could imagine, there was more than one argument over whether the shot actually hit you or whether the shooter missed. Occasionally, we sought a decision from a "judge" (one of the adults), but they would usually say, "If you can't play without arguing, you won't be playing at all!"

As fun as that game was, it only lasted while my relatives were with us that one summer. We tried to play it once after they left, but it just was not the same, so we put down our cap guns and never played it again! Go figure!

Golfing. Another craze that captured our attention was golfing. I don't mean "real golfing" - I mean the kind of golfing we played with plastic golf balls and holes that we dug in the yard. You can still buy these plastic golf balls for practicing your golf swing. I know because I just bought a dozen pack for my four-pound Yorkie puppy, Bella. She does not play golf, but she does like to chew on them.

I think there were nine "holes" in the Garnett golf course – nine, so as to give the feeling that we were playing "real golf." There was no "front nine" or "back nine;" there was just "*the* nine."

There was also no putting because there were no greens on which to putt. One could only chip shots with his "irons". I remember one hole was a particularly good one in that you had to chip the ball over the roof of our house to get to the hole. You could not, of course, see the hole when you shot, so it created a great deal of curiosity to see just where the ball landed as you rounded the corner of the house.

The nine holes were laid out by my big brother, Howard, and everyone agreed that he had a real gift for golf course architecture. That would be everyone except our new neighbors, Ike and Sally Farley.

It seems that Howard felt the golf course needed to extend beyond the boundaries of our own yard, so he expanded the course into the boundaries of the Farley's yard. I don't think Ike and Sally would have minded us being in their yard per se, but they were not particularly fond of the holes Howard dug in their new sod! Their concerned, expressed to my parents, resulted in the reduction of our golf course from nine holes to seven holes.

For a while, we played golf almost everyday that summer. We played with each other and by ourselves, constantly comparing our scores. Being the youngest, I don't believe I ever turned in the lowest score, but looking back I see now that I should have received a "handicap" at least a couple of strokes for being the youngest and smallest. But as Rodney Dangerfield used to say, I never "got any respect!"

This craze ended too, but it prepared us for the superb golfers we were in later years when we would travel together to a par three golf course over by Norwalk. My brother would drive his 1960 white Corvair (with the two carburetors), and the three of us would spend an afternoon playing "real golf" together.

This is the time and place that my sister, Pat, earned her title, "The Helicopter." That seemed an appropriate title for her in light of the fact that, after hitting a bad shot, she often would throw her club down the fairway in true "helicopter-like fashion." In other words, the management of the course did not relish seeing the Garnett kids coming for an afternoon of "real golf."

Later, my golfing career was stunted after taking a golf class under Donald Kingsbury in high school. I told everyone not to hit their balls until I retrieved my balls that were 100 yards down course. When I stooped down to pick up my first ball, Larry Newman (a fellow classmate) drove his ball anyway, and it hit me right in the shin!

Murder did not seem an appropriate response although I did entertain the thought, so I just yelled at him instead. That incident affected my golf game for years to come – in that I was always a bit nervous on the fairways and was constantly looking to see if any balls were coming my direction! I think that fear most likely was the greatest contributing factor to my poor scores. Others thought lack of talent could be involved, but I knew Larry Newman was responsible. In fact, there is no telling how good a golfer I might have been had it not been for him hitting his ball at me – maybe even a Pro?

Home Run Derby. Somewhere around 1959 or 1960, there was a popular TV show called Home Run Derby. It featured professional baseball players who would compete against each other in an attempt to see who could hit the most home runs. Any hit except a home run was called an out, so the nine innings went really fast. I remember watching both the great Mickey Mantle and the great Roger Maris (who hit 61 home runs for the New York Yankees in 1961 breaking Babe Ruth's record of 60 set in 1927) appear on the show. If my memory serves me correctly, neither of them won the Home Run Derby contest when they appeared.

So, the Garnett kids took their cue from this popular TV show and held their own Home Run Derby right in our front yard with a plastic ball and bat. The batter would stand up near the section on the east side of house where there were no windows, and use the house as a backstop. The pitcher would pitch the plastic wiffle ball from the pitcher's mound (there actually was no mound) about 30 feet from the batter. The row of Mom's peonies that bordered the east side of the yard was the home run fence.

Everything except the ball going over the peonies in the air was an out. Three outs to an inning made things move right along.

As I shut my eyes and think back to those "derby days," I can hear the locusts singing in the large oak tree that sat in the neighbor's yard just to the east of us. It is funny that I do not remember taking note of them at the time, but their singing was evidently an integral part of the activities because as I close my eyes and see us playing, I can hear them as clear as day.

One summer we played "Home Run Derby" just about every day, then for whatever reason, we lost interest in that game and rarely picked up the bat and ball thereafter.

The Dart Game. I had all but forgotten about the summer we got a dart game, but my sister, Pat, asked me (out of fear) if I was going to include it my stories. You will see in a moment why she "hoped" that I would not, but her mention of it demands that I share it with you so the truth can come out into the daylight.

This dart game was a 36" round dartboard with chrome dividers between the sections. The darts were about seven inches long, made of wood with a 4" steel point. Obviously, it did not have sticker on it that said it was "for kids of a certain age." This dart game could not have been for kids – unless it was for the Adams family or the Manson family!

The first day we got the game is the only day I remember playing with it. Pat was sitting on the front porch and was looking at the dartboard. I picked up one of the darts and said to her, "Hold up the board, and I will see if I can hit it."

It never occurred to me (nor to her) that it was not a real good idea to hold up a dartboard as someone throws darts at it – especially darts made of wood with a 4" steel tip.

Not wanting to throw the dart with a lot of force, I sort of lobbed it in the air. I saw immediately that more force should have been applied, because the dart looped up in the air, came short of the dartboard, and stuck in my sister's ankle. That had to leave a mark!

I am sure there must have been other days we played darts, but I cannot remember any. There is a distinct possibility that after the first day's experience, the dartboard found a new home.

The Isometric Bar. Then there was the summer where my brother was talking about a great new exercise program the coach was promoting. It was called "isometrics."

Wikipedia defines isometrics as "a type of strength training in which the joint angle and muscle length do not change during contraction (compared to concentric or eccentric contractions, called dynamic/isotonic movements). Isometrics are done in static positions, rather than being dynamic through a range of motion."

In layman's terms, this translates to pushing or pulling against an immoveable bar while grinding your teeth until your face turns red and the veins in your neck pop out.

Our isometric exercise bar consisted of two 10' long, 2' x 6's set vertically into concrete. The two 2 x 6's were drilled full of 2" inch holes about every 3 inches.

When one wished to engage in isometric exercise, he inserted the 2" steel pole through a hole in one 2 x 6 and lined it up with a corresponding hole in the other 2 x 6. The height of the horizontal steel pole dictated whether you were to push down or pull up.

Nothing moved while you were engaging in this high tech strength innovation except maybe your eyebrows or your jaws. The idea was "force meeting resistance will result in strength." Had I become acquainted with this piece of equipment as an adult, I would insist that it have a warning label stuck on it that reads "Will Likely Produce Hemorrhoids."

It was really quite a project for my grandpa Fred to construct. Unfortunately, I think it took him longer to build it than the time we actually used it. It held our interest no more than three weeks.

That is so interesting because it stood in our yard for at least 20 years. Maybe Mom and Dad thought they would start using it some day after we kids left home? Or maybe they hoped it would lure us back home again? I know for a fact that it stood there long after anyone could remember where the steel pole had disappeared.

Although my memories of actually using the isometric bar are few, the fondest of those memories occurred the very day it "opened for business." My dad, who at that time was in his forties, boldly proclaimed that he could still "skin the cat" as he used to do as a kid on the playground. Skinning the cat is an exercise where one hangs from the bar, pulls one's legs up and through one's arms, then reverses the move from that inverted position and undoes what he just did.

To my amazement, my dad did as he said he would do. He "skinned the cat" that day on the isometric bar. My older brother was able to duplicate the move, but I think I had something in my eye and could not attempt it that day. Later, when no one was around, I tried to do it, and fell on my head. But who cares if you can "skin the cat" or not? That has always been my attitude toward those things I cannot do. It just makes life easier as opposed to thinking you are a failure.

Wham-O's. One craze that lasted far longer than all the others would be that of the flying "wham-o's." Today that are called Frisbee's, but at the first they were called "wham-o's" because they were made by the Wham-O Corporation (it said so right on the edge of the wham-o).

In August of that year we went to the Iowa State Fair and had our first exposure to these flying wonders. There were two men across the street from "Ye Old Mill" who demonstrated amazing things one could do with a wham-o. You could curve them through the branches of a tree, you could skip them on the ground, you could make them act like a boomerang and come back to you, or you could make them fly straight as an arrow (as in playing catch).

We were so taken with how much fun these guys were having, we bought three wham-o's, a red one, a yellow one, and a green one. Mine was the red one, and it was the best of the bunch (an interesting brag in light of the fact that all three were exactly alike in every detail).

These were no flimsy, fly-by-night, put together wham-o's! They were heavy duty, thick plastic orbs that were built to last! We knew at a moment's glance that they were good investments.

The Garnett kids, if I say so myself, became quite proficient with our wham-o's. We could make them curve, skip, boomerang, or fly straight as an arrow.

And they were extremely durable! We discovered this fact after our dog, Peaches, found the wham-o's one day and chewed on them. They had been so skillfully made that even her tooth marks could not make them wobble in flight.

The most notable event that proved the value of these flying orbs was the vacation we took to Missouri. There, we stayed in a friend's house for one entire week with absolutely, positively nothing to do. It may have been restful for my folks, but it was an excruciating week for us kids. Had it not been for the suggestion of our mom to toss our wham-o's into the car trunk before we left home, I am absolutely sure we would have died from boredom!

We had those wham-o's for at least 15 years. I even remember seeing one of them in my closet on a return trip to home when I was in my thirties! That, my friend, is longevity!

Hula Hoops. Because the Garnett kids were always on the cutting edge of whatever was popular (not!), we all three had "hula hoops."

I do not remember how we were introduced to them, but each of us also became quite proficient in our use of our hoop. Not only could we "hula" them around our waists, but we could also throw them with an underhand spinning motion way ahead of us, and watch them "walk" back to us. We transformed our hula-hoops into an offshoot of the boomerang, and normally left onlookers in awe.

I was shocked to read recently about the popularity of the hula hoop: *"Invented in 1957, by an Australian, the name "hula hoop" came from the Hawaiian dance its users seemed to imitate. The invention was licensed to the Wham-O Corporation, who sold* **25 million hula-hoops in two months***. Almost 100 million international orders followed. They were manufacturing 20,000 hoops a day at the peak of popularity. Not all nations thought this was such a spiffy idea. Japan banned the hoops thinking they might promote improprieties. The Soviet Union said the hula-hoop was an example of the "emptiness of American culture."* (www.crazyfads.com/50's)

You may own a "Wii Fit" game that is played on the Wii video game console as you stand on the Wii Fitness Board? One of their exercises had been made much easier for those of us who grew up with the Hula Hoop. As you "hula" your imaginary hoop around your midsection, you see the corresponding little Wii person on the screen rotating their Hula Hoop around their waste. That exercise brings back many memories of "hula-ing" as a child. I might add that it is much easier to rotate an imaginary hula-hoop in the Wii Fit program, than to keep your hula-hoop spinning with a real one.

Out of curiosity I just Googled "purchase a hula hoop" to see if a person could buy one today, and got 2,900,000 "results." Apparently, the hula-hoop is still popular more than 50 years after its invention.

Chapter Fourteen

Halloween In Carlisle

Halloween in the little Iowa town of Carlisle was something that I always looked forward to. You may be surprised if I told you why. It was the smell.

Yes, that does sound a bit goofy, but in my case it is goofy and true. I loved the smell of Halloween! The best way to describe the smell would be "damp leaves."

I remember one evening on Halloween in Carlisle it had rained early in the evening, and then it cleared off. As I was walking in an unlit area of town, I was thinking to myself, "Boy, this is cool! I am out here all by myself, it has stopped raining, it is warm, and it smells really good!" It smelled sort of like being in a forest - damp, and cool, and refreshing.

That "smell" was generated by the fall leaves on the ground dampened by the earlier rain. In fact, this experience was duplicated and reinforced later in life as an adult as I escorted my kids from house to house when they were little. It had rained earlier that evening too, and the ground was wet, and smelled like damp leaves. I remember thinking, "This smells just like it did when I was a kid in Carlisle." So, to me, it makes perfect sense – Halloween is associated with the smell of damp leaves.

In the 1950's we did not go to the store and buy a Halloween costume like kids do today. In fact, I don't believe I ever saw a Halloween costume that had been purchased at the store in my childhood. Kids who were planning on "trick or treating" had been discussing with their parents for days what they "wanted to be" that night. Some of their parents had made costumes for them, especially the girls.

For some reason, in my early years I chose the option to go trick or treating as a "hobo." I think I liked that occupation because I got to have a "beard" for the evening. True, it was drawn on with a mascara pencil, but it looked real – at least through the eyes of a little boy. I was sure no one would know who I was because the beard made me look so much older!

We knew we had good "disguises" when our neighbors could not guess who we were, or at least they said they did not know. As we went out their door, we usually told them who we were, and they were so "surprised" to see we lived near them.

It was absolutely required to tell a joke or say something funny before you received your treat. You would never think of walking up to a door and getting candy without making those people laugh with your funny little joke. It never occurred to me that, by the time I knocked on their door, they had heard my little joke about the "biggest pencil in the world" or the "car in the oven" a good 40 times already. They acted like it was the first time they had ever heard it, and laughed like they really thought it was funny.

In those days there was little education about the "evils" of candy. Most people did not eat an abundance of sweets because they did not have the money to buy them, not because they thought it was bad for them. So, once we filled up our bags (big bags) with free candy, we were allowed to eat everything we collected.

After all three of us kids came back to our house, we would dump our bag of candy on the living room floor and trade with each other. Believe it or not, there were some items that one did not like but the others did, and visa versa so the swap at the end worked out really well.

Two distinct memories come to mind about my "Halloweening" days in Carlisle. One memory has to do with the older lady down the street who was giving out candy bars – my favorite candy bars! That was a pretty big treat for those days. It just did not seem right that I could only have *one* of these. They were free and I liked them so much! Plus, I knew my brother or sister would definitely not trade their candy bar to me, so I did what any candy bar-liking-little-kid would do – I devised a way to get two of them!

After going to her door, telling my joke, and receiving my candy bar, I hid around the corner of her house out of sight for about 10 minutes. Then I pulled my jacket over my head, and went back for "seconds." I dropped my voice down into a lower register (actually an eight year old does not have much of a lower register), and selected a different joke from my repertoire of jokes. I was extremely pleased that she was "completed fooled" into giving me another candy bar – or at least she acted like she was completely fooled. She was friends with my folks, and I wonder now, if she didn't think "little

Jimmie Garnett was so cute in coming back a second time." Do you think that could be possible?

The other Halloween memory has to do with what was in my pocket. I must have been in 6th grade the night I grabbed a handful of carrot sticks as I left the house to trick or treat. Without thinking, I stuck them in my jacket pocket, the same jacket pocket that I had previously put a bar of soap. Why on earth would I have a bar of soap in my pocket? That is because the meanest, dirtiest, most underhanded Halloween "trick" one could receive was to have his house or car windows "soaped." Having them "soaped" simply means someone took a bar of soap and rubbed over the window. The soap, you see, does not clean off easily. This action was reserved for someone you did not particularly care for, or it could be used on total strangers.

After being out for about 30 minutes, I remembered the carrot sticks, so I reached in my pocket, grabbed one, and bit off a big piece. Would it surprise you to know that it tasted like soap? It was absolutely, positively, awful! I spit out the whole mouthful of carrots, and just kept spitting on-and-off for at least an hour. That soap taste just would not go away.

Later on in the evening, I forgot about the first carrot, and popped another piece of carrot in my mouth. It tasted just as bad the first one – absolutely, positively awful! I then threw the rest of the carrots away!

But here's the worst part: for years to come – that's right, *literally for years to come* – every carrot I tried, tasted like soap! I have concluded that the mind must be a powerful thing to be able to transform every carrot I tasted for years into soap!

Even today, if I do not think about the fact that the present carrot has not come into any contact with a bar of soap, I can taste soap when I eat a carrot!

This strange mysterious phenomenon would then make one wonder what would have happened had my carrots rubbed up against a piece of chocolate candy, or a piece of pizza, or some butter pecan ice cream? It really makes one wonder, doesn't it?

Anyway, looking back to Halloween in Carlisle brings back such good memories for me, and for the little boy who still lives inside.

Chapter Fifteen

Rolling Down Hills

Most of today's crowd would classify the Garnett kids as "extremely boring" if they knew that one our favorite activities was to roll down hills.

This exciting activity began for me before age 4 at my grandpa and grandma's house on the north side of Carlisle. Their yard had a hill in it. Although the hill was only 6 feet long and not very steep, it was a hill to a little 4-year-old boy. This hill served to connect the upper yard with the lower yard.

There were times when we visited their home and didn't partake in this exciting practice of rolling down their hill, but it was not unusual to do so. I am sure my excitement was the result of my brother and sister's excitement, because frankly, I never really thought it was a lot of fun. At times it made me feel sick to my stomach.

My folks had some friends out in the country by the

name of Mott who lived on Scotch Ridge Road. Their house sat off from the road quite a ways and was about 60 feet higher than the road that passed by. This created a big hill between their house and the road. It was steep, and it was long.

Whenever Mom said she was going to the Mott's to get apples, us three kids were in the car before she got her baskets out of the smokehouse.

Because this hill was so big and so steep, it was difficult for us to roll down it without going sideways and coming to a complete stop. This was not bad, necessarily, because if one continued to roll down "Mott's hill" all at one time, you would have hit speeds up to at least one zillion miles an hour!

I doubt that many of today's kids have much desire to roll down hills, at least I have not seen many kids rolling down hills lately, in fact, none. It is interesting that activities of "yesteryear" often seem to have little to offer today's kids. I know my grandma Mabel could never understand why we were not real excited to play one of her favorite childhood games – "shinny." As I understood it, the gist of that game was to hit a can down the road with a stick. Her excitement about playing shinny never caught fire in our hearts either, so maybe rolling down hills is kind of like that?

It makes you wonder what games the kids of the future will consider fun. Obviously, neither shinny nor rolling down hills.

Stop the presses! After commenting on today's kids not being interested in rolling down hills, I have to admit that my assumption was completely wrong! We just returned from a weekend in the Quad Cities where we spent time with one set of our grandchildren at a local park in Milan, Il.

As we drove into the park area, I noticed it was surrounded on three sides by some very large hills. I looked to the left to see a group of children, apparently a daycare class, standing at the top of one of the hills. At their teacher's signal, groups of four or five kids began rolling down the hill, and they were having a ball!

A few minutes later, my three year old granddaughter ran up the hill with her dad, and I watched them both roll down the hill together!

So, my analysis of the current sentiment of today's youth toward rolling down hills could not have been more incorrect. They appear to have the same fire and passion for rolling down hills as the Garnett children of yesteryear had.

My faith in today's youth has been restored. It makes me wonder if they also like to play shinny? Grandma Mabel would be pleased.

Chapter Sixteen

The School Playground

On a warm July afternoon, when I was around 9 years old, I decided to ride my bike down to the elementary school playground. After all, it was my favorite place to be for nine months of the year – not the school, but the playground. It was only a block from our house, so it would be convenient. I thought to myself as I rode my bike down the sidewalk, "I am not sure why I hadn't thought of coming here before. This will be my first of many trips down here."

The Carlisle High School faced School Street on the north with the elementary school building to the south. The playground was just to the east of the elementary building. This is the same elementary building, by the way, that was the home of the famed "Roller Derby" contests for the skating Garnett kids.

In order to reach the playground area you took the sidewalk that went between the gymnasium (attached to the high school) and a separate building to the east that housed the boiler for the school. Because this building was separate from the high school building, the upstairs was used for band, chorus, and art.

The sidewalk made a slight incline just before passing between these two buildings, and then leveled off so you could see the playground down below. That playground held a lot of fond memories for me - memories of playing "red rover, red rover," "king of the hill," swinging on the swings, sliding on the slide, playing dodge ball, basketball, and riding the merry-go-round.

The Old Carlisle High School

There it stood in all of its splendor, just like it looked during the school year. Taking the sidewalk down the hill you first encountered the basketball court, then the tetherball court, then the jungle gym, then the slide, then the swings to the left, and then the merry-go-round.

I remember wondering why I had not taken advantage of coming to the playground before this. After all, I would have it all to myself now. There would be no standing in line to use the slide or the swings, which was always the case at recess. I could do what I wanted, when I wanted, and as many times as I wanted! This was going to be fun!

I circled the playground once to determine what activity I should embark on first. I decided to swing first because you always had to stand in line to secure one of the six swings. I chose swing number six cause it had earned the reputation of being the "best one." Then I did swing number two, then four, and before long, I had swung in every one of the swings. This was really neat!

But a peculiar thing happened then – swinging just did not seem to have the "fun" to it as it did during recess time. In fact, neither did the slide, nor the merry-go-round, nor the tetherball, nor the jungle gym. In fact, the playground was quite a different play when you were there all by yourself.

It was then I noticed that during the summer months, a few mournful shoots of grass had grown up in the cracks of the blacktop. It gave the playground a sort of lonely, desolate feel.

There seemed to be a certain "ingredient" missing today on the school playground, and that ingredient was the other kids. With them, it was fun, without them it was not.

I look back now and see that July afternoon on the school playground was teaching me a lesson about life. Many, if not *most*, of the things in life are constructed in such a way that they are better enjoyed with someone else. It is not the objects themselves that are fun, but the *sharing* of those objects with other people that make the experience what it is.

After that one warm July afternoon, I never went back to the playground by myself during the summer months. It just was not the same.

I do remember though, that during a recess the following fall, I remembered my trip to the playground on that warm July afternoon. I glanced around the playground and thought how different it felt to be there with it full of kids versus when I was by myself.

From then on, I never complained about having to stand in line to get a swing or go down the slide. The crowded playground was what made the playground fun!

Chapter Seventeen
Staying All Night At Grandma's

My grandma Mabel was the best grandma ever! She was so kind and sweet, and always had time for us. She would even plan special things for us to do when we visited her.

Grandma and Grandpa's House on
Pennsylvania Avenue in Carlisle

Occasionally, one of us would get to spend the night with her and Grandpa Fred. They did not live far away, just on the north side of Carlisle about a block from the city park. Today their house stands across the street from the family who put Carlisle on the map – the McCaughey's – known for their septuplets. During my childhood, an old dilapidated house sat where their house now sits. The McCaughey's house is a fine improvement over the former landscape.

It was nice spending the night with Grandma and Grandpa. Grandpa Fred usually did not enter into the festivities that Grandma planned for us kids, but I am sure he enjoyed having us over too.

Grandma created exciting things for us to do. She would have us write a note and stick it in an empty bottle. We would then bury the bottle somewhere in the yard. Within an hour or two, we would go dig up the bottle and pretend that we had found an important note in an ancient bottle buried for centuries!

Then she would have us roast marshmallows on a long hairpin over our own little candle, and one time she built a little fireplace out of a couple of bricks, then cooked our lunch on it. Grandma did so many things with us like play cards and play games, and she actually acted like she enjoyed doing it.

Probably the best thing Grandma did was to give us back rubs. To be accurate, she didn't actually *rub* your back; she just sort of ran her fingers over it. It was a most relaxing experience for us. I do the same thing to my little four-pound Yorkie puppy. She rolls on her back, stretches her legs, and waits for me to rub her belly. And when I do, she goes into some kind of Nirvana experience, just like we used to do when Grandma rubbed our backs.

Often Grandma would close her eyes and lay her head back. I remember trying to figure out if she was asleep. I guess she was not because she continued to rub my back, and I don't think she could have done that if she were asleep. She always told me she was just "resting her eyes," but I learned later in life that that can mean one is asleep but does not want to admit it.

Everything was great when we stayed all night at Grandma Mabel's house, *until it was time to go to bed.* Grandma and Grandpa's bedroom was just off the kitchen at one end of the house. Our bedroom was just off the living room at the opposite end of the house. I have to tell you, that bedroom was spooky! It had a triple threat:

Grandpa and Grandma
Garnett
50th Wedding Anniversary
Circa 1963

(1) The Closet. Yes, the bedroom had a closet right next to the bed. The closet had a light that hung from a cord and turned on with a pull string. The light must have been a "25 watt-er," because it did not light up the closet much. It only gave it a shadowy affect. I always took a quick look in the closet before I jumped in the bed to make sure nothing was hiding in it, but once I closed that door, I had no idea what might come alive inside, ready to spring out at me the moment I closed my eyes.

(2) **The Shadows on the Wall.** Outside Grandma's house on the corner of the street, was a street light that was a giant bulb sitting beneath a big green metal shade which was painted white on the under side. That streetlight made the night come alive inside the bedroom by casting shadows on the wall as its light passed through the venetian blinds on the window. One had the choice of sleeping with those shadows on the wall or closing the blinds, making the bedroom even darker. I always chose to leave the blinds open and deal with the shadows.

(3) **The Alarm Clock.** Sitting on Grandpa's dresser in their bedroom was a huge windup alarm clock. That clock never drew attention to itself until the lights were turned off, and I was in bed by myself. Then that clock took on a personality of its own.

Every time I closed my eyes, I could hear that methodical "tick, tick, tick" *coming down the hallway and getting closer to my room*. The "ticks" would get louder the closer it came, until I took the only option that a young boy was given! I said in a forlorn voice, "Grandma, I can't go to sleep. Can you sleep with me for a while?"

I always hated to have to resort to that option, but what was a guy to do? I had to keep my eyelids open or something would open the closet door and grab me, or the alarm clock would reach its final destination right beside my bed, or those shadows on the wall would suddenly reveal a new shadow – the monster that was going to get me!

Grandma would always come in and lie by me and rub my back until I went to sleep. She was a good Grandma. And she never told my brother or sister about having to come in and lie with me. They would have made fun of me.

It was not until many years later that I discovered my older brother and my older sister were also scared to stay in that bedroom and used the very same technique to lure Grandma to the bedroom so they could go to sleep too.

Grandma's house was fun – all except that bedroom after dark. It was spooky! Even today, when the light shines through our venetian blinds and casts shadows in our bedroom, I think of Grandma's bedroom and spending the night with her.

Chapter Eighteen

Thursday Night Quarterback Club

I loved playing football! Our team had been together since Junior High days, and we worked together like a well-oiled machine! Each of us loved winning, but we also loved the game itself. Because our school was small, I played fullback on offense and linebacker on defense.

In my high school days we had three coaches: John Bankus was our head coach, Dick Armstrong and Fred Smith were his assistants. These men were men of integrity and character, and they loved the game of football too! They also loved to win, which we did most often.

Special mention would have to be given to Coach Smith for the "rock concert" he provided the team. Yes, rock concert! One morning he announced that our football team would be excused from all afternoon classes to attend a "rock concert." Our excitement diminished when we realized that meant we were going to crawl around on our hands and knees all afternoon in the hot sun picking up rocks from our new football field. Rock concert, my foot!

I felt highly honored after summer morning practice, when Coach Bankus caught me alone and asked me if I would help him move something out of his apartment. I really felt special. That something was a refrigerator that needed to be moved out of the building from his third floor apartment.

I am so grateful that Coach did not hold grudges. You see, he was on the bottom end of the refrigerator as we were going down the stairs when, from the topside, I lost my grip. The refrigerator sort of pushed him down the stairs and into the wall on the second stairs landing. He was not hurt, thankfully, but my pride certainly was! I wished he had asked someone else to help him after that happened!

I saw Coach Bankus at my dad's funeral in 2001. It was really great to see him again, but I thought it a bit unfair that he had hardly aged! After shaking hands and greeting each other, he asked me if I remembered the night we played Interstate 35? Of course I did! The coaches had told us that this was the team that could beat us, so we were pumped for that game! On our first offensive play from scrimmage, the linemen opened up a hole for me that a Mack truck could have driven through! I was able to score a touchdown virtually untouched from the 52-yard line! We went on to beat them 52 to 0! We loved football! We also loved winning!

But there was something else I loved about football season – the Thursday night Quarterback Club meetings. This was the night the fathers and friends of the football team met together to watch the films of the last game. And, oh yes, to eat donuts and drink chocolate milk.

I can remember the excitement as I would walk to school for the meeting, having left early so I could chat with other members of the team before it started. I have to say to you, as I close my eyes and think back, I can feel the excitement once again.

As I analyzed why the meeting was so important to me, I came up with these answers: (1) my dad would tell me how proud he was of me, (2) we almost always won by a huge margin so the game films were enjoyable, (3) it was like playing the game again, (4) and I liked donuts and chocolate milk.

There was one Thursday night meeting though that I was a bit hesitant to attend. I had done something extremely stupid during the preceding game and was afraid it had been caught on film for all to see. I did not share my fear with anyone, for then I would have had to draw attention to what I had done, so I just sweat bullets as the game film started to play.

In the second half of that game, we kicked off to the other team after scoring. I was also on the kickoff team as well as playing fullback and linebacker. I recall running down the sideline nearest the stands (and nearest the coaches) in hot pursuit of the guy who was about to catch the kickoff. No one was near me, and I was running as fast I could. I was ready to tackle this guy hard enough to make him cough up the ball upon impact. I could see it all taking place - I hit him hard and low, he fumbles the ball, my name is announced over the PA system, and I am a hero!

Unfortunately, that never occurred because for some unexplained reason, I tripped and fell right on my face – in front of the stands and in front of the coaches. Understand, no one tripped me – I just tripped over my own feet!

Of course I jumped to my feet immediately, praying to God that every eye had been focused on the guy who had caught the ball, and not me falling on my face for no earthly reason!

I started breathing hard as the game film drew near to this part of the game. Oh, no, there it was on the film! I saw myself running all by myself, and then for no reason, I fell flat on my face – right in front of the stands and right in front of the coaches.

I prayed that no one else in the room noticed what I had done. No one said anything about it, so I thought I was home free! God had miraculously blinded the eyes of everyone in the room, and they missed seeing my stupid stunt.

The film continued and our team brought the runner down. We were now beyond that section, and I could breathe easy. Then I heard Coach Bankus say, "But wait just a minute! Did you see what I just saw?" Then he ran the projector back to just before we kicked off, and instructed the Thursday Quarterback Club crowd to "watch Garnett as he executes a very unusual play strategy here."

There I was in all of my glory, falling flat on my face, for no earthly reason! Of course everyone laughed when they saw me fall – everyone but me. What an idiot! I found out later that the coaches had seen me fall the first time they watched the film and planned on pointing it out to the crowd that night! Was that teacher abuse or what?

Thursday night Quarterback Club - It was a delightful time that I could spend with my dad, watching something I loved to do, being with my friends, and eating donuts and chocolate milk.

Thank you Coach Bankus, Coach Armstrong, and Coach Smith for what you taught me about football, about myself, and about life. Your influence went way beyond the four walls of a classroom. You played an instrumental role in my life, not just in building an athlete, but in building a man.

1968 Carlisle Wildcats Football Team

"As far as is known this is one of the most successful Wildcat squads in history. The Wildcats were able to grind out 2,578 yards rushing, compared to their opponents 302...The Wildcats rolled up a total of 297 points while limiting their foes to 60."

- 1968 Wildcat Annual

I am in the second row, second from the left. Please note the wavy hair!

Chapter Nineteen
"When The Cat's Away..."

I do not know how this practice got started, and I do not know what brought it to an end, but for a while as I was growing up, there was a lot of excitement when Mom and Dad left the house to go on an errand.

We three kids would look out the window until we were absolutely sure our parents' car had left the driveway and was heading down the street. It was then, and only then, that we made a mad dash to the refrigerator!

It was not that we were malnourished (if you knew me, you would know how ludicrous that thought is) or that we were being starved by our folks. In fact, we were not even hungry. We were simply intent on enjoying a greater quantity of a few food items that we apparently felt we were not getting enough of. That would be Hershey's chocolate, Pet milk, and maraschinos cherries. These were the three items on our target list.

The Hershey's chocolate that Mom bought came in a can that opened with a metal can opener punch. One end of the opener was for opening pop bottles, and the other end was for punching a triangle shaped hole in the top of a can. This hole made it possible for a pretty good sized  flow of chocolate syrup to be poured out of the can. The hole also enabled a pretty good sized flow of chocolate syrup to run into your mouth if you were "drinking out of the can" like I did.

Usually one gulp was all a kid could handle because it was so sweet. We had no fear of "drinking" after each other, and what we three kids did to that can of Hershey's was similar to what our North Carolina kinfolk did to a jug of their "white lightening." In other words, each of us lowered the quantity of the liquid significantly!

The second item that we focused on was the bottle of maraschinos cherries. I do not remember why Mom had a bottle of those, but I would guess they were for baking. I believe these are they same type of cherries that are inside "chocolate covered cherries." They are absolutely delicious, but they, too, are extremely sweet. They go through some sort of a process that makes them much sweeter than a normal cherry.

Mom used another type of cherry when she made cherry pie. She and Dad always played a little game when she made one of these pies. Dad would take a bite, make a face, and say, "Sally, these are too sour!" and Mom would reply, "Lyle, I put a whole cup of sugar in that pie!" One would think that after playing out that scenario 50 times, it would not have been too exciting, but it happened every single time she baked a cherry pie.

I do not remember if we showed restraint and only took one cherry, or if we each took two or three. There could not have been over 25 cherries in the little jar, so I imagine we each tried to be satisfied with just one. After all, we did not want to make it obvious that we had raided these goodies while Mom and Dad were gone. Right!

The third item we attacked was the Pet evaporated milk. Actually, I cannot say for sure if Howard and Pat liked it or not, but I know I surely did. It came in a can, about the same size as the Hershey's chocolate can, and was opened with a can opener punch that left a pretty big triangular whole which allowed this a fairly good swallow.

.

Wikipedia explains, "John Baptist Meÿenberg (1847-1914) was an operator at the Anglo-Swiss milk condensery at Cham, Switzerland. Anglo-Swiss made sweetened condensed milk. From 1866 through 1883, Meÿenberg experimented with preservation of milk without the use of sugar. He discovered that condensed milk would last longer if heated to 120°C (248°F) in a sealed container, and hence could be preserved without adding sugar." As soon as the can was opened, then it required refrigeration and that is why we found it in the fridge.

I think its main purpose was to be used in baking, but I preferred it for just straight drinking. I remember it to be a little "thicker" than our regular milk was (which was whole milk), but the taste was more like sweet cream.

I do not remember Mom or Dad ever asking any of us if we had raided these items, but I cannot imagine they were not aware that we were getting into them while they were gone.

I still like all three of these items and would "sample" them if they were in our refrigerator. I have not had a taste of Pet milk for many years, but even yesterday as Ginny and I dined at a local restaurant, I opened the little plastic containers of cold half and half, and drank four or five of them. Oh – did I mention to you that I like cream?

Chapter Twenty

Mid 50's and Early 60's Fads

Wikipedia says *"A fad is any form of behavior that develops among a large population and is collectively followed enthusiastically for a period of time, generally as a result of the behavior being perceived as popular by one's peers or being deemed 'cool' by social media. A fad is said to "catch on" when the number of people adopting it begins to increase rapidly. The behavior will normally fade quickly once the perception of novelty is gone."*

No one who knows me would ever call me "fad conscious," now or then. As I look back to those childhood days, I am able to be more observant now of the fads that took place than I ever was at that time. So, let me name the few fads of "my day" that I am aware of.

Cuffed Jeans. Kids back in the 50's bought their jeans long enough to turn up the pant legs and cuff them. I did not know this was a fad; I just knew that if my big brother did it, I was going to do it.

Buying jeans was a humiliating thing for me. The sales lady at JC Penney's would take one look at me, then say to my mom, "Let's see now, you will want to go to the 'husky' section to look for his jeans."

"Husky section" - that was not a compliment. Translated into "little boy language" it meant, "You need to go to the *fat boy* section to get his jeans because he couldn't possibly wear normal ones!" I am sure it was not meant to be mean, but that is how I interpreted it. I hated to go jean buying!

Heel Plates. Heel plates, or "taps" as we called them, were little curved pieces of metal that fastened to the edge of the heels of your shoes. Their purpose was to stop your heels from wearing down quicker than the rest of your shoe. I am sure they accomplished that goal, but they also had another purpose – to make a lot of noise when you walked down the school hallways.

Can you imagine walking down the hard surfaced hallway with steel taps on your heels? You could be heard a mile away! You would not be sneaking up on anyone anytime soon!

I am sure that some kids would have been embarrassed beyond measure to make so much noise as they walked down the hallway, but I, for one, liked it. You could hear every single step very distinctly. It sounded like a horse wearing horseshoes dancing on a marble floor!

And best of all, I got to have these "taps" on my new pair of black shoes that had a pop-up buckle clip on them. This buckle clip covered the shoe tongue. You raised the buckle clip up to put your shoes on, then you pushed it down to make your shoe secure on your feet. It was cool!

Flat Tops and Butch Wax. My brother and I sported "crew cuts" when I was in preteen years. The "crew cut," also called a "flat top" made the top of your head perfectly flat. My head was big so it resembled the deck of an aircraft carrier.

Of course one's hair needed some "assistance" in its attempt to stand straight up. That did not occur naturally, so you purchased a jar of "butch wax." You had two choices, Lucky Tiger or the cheaper brand that had a plastic long-toothed hand comb for a lid. You could slip your third finger through the convenient, built- in, ring-type handle on the comb, and you were all set. Dab some goo into your hair, and comb it in with backward strokes. And before long, it was standing to attention – straight up!

This stuff was extremely sticky and made it difficult to separate your fingers from each other. I know, because I usually got it all over my hands and was not real fond of having to wash them! It was worth it though, my hair stood straight and tall. I think it would have withstood gale force winds from a hurricane!

It seems appropriate to mention this while we are on the subject of hair. Somewhere along the line, my older brother Howard was told it would be good for your hair (and your "cool factor") to put Vaseline in it. Frankly, I never did quite understand what benefit the Vaseline added, but little brothers do as their older brothers do. So I put Vaseline in my hair too. I think the next step after applying a goodly amount of Vaseline, was to wash your hair. In other words, you washed out the very stuff that you had just put in! Go figure.

If this fad caught on in other households, we were not

aware of it. I stopped using this hair treatment when Howard stopped using it, which I believe was after a week or two. I do not remember any comments made during that time as to how good, or how shiny, or how reflective our hair looked. That's probably why it never caught on in Carlisle circles.

Color-Coordinated Shirts and Socks. I am thinking that this fad hit during my Junior High years. I remember buying a yellow shirt with yellow socks, a pink (yes pink) shirt with pink socks, and a lime green shirt with lime green socks. One thing was for sure – you could see me coming! I eventually kept the shirts and threw away the stupid colored socks!

Tie-Dye Shirts. These shirts were T-shirts that were crumpled, folded, twisted, or pleated, then dyed. The dye would only reach certain portions of the shirt, so one was left with unusual patterns of color on the shirt. Here is an example of one. Tie-dye shirts have apparently made a resurgence today, because the Internet  is full of places to buy them and instructions on how to make your own.

Madrus Shirts. These shirts of the early 60's were typically a plaid pattern that used non-colorfast dyes that "bled" each time the shirt was washed. These "bleeding Madrus" shirts would potentially produce a new color combination with each washing. (I wonder what happened if you had a tendency to sweat a lot? Did the non-colorfast dye "bleed" out all over your body?) I do not remember owning one of these.

Matching Couples Shirts. These were two identical shirts (except for size) worn at the same time by a couple. It made a bold statement to everyone who saw you together –

"We Are A Couple." These were especially popular with couples who were extremely jealous and possessive of each other. I mean why on earth would you ever make a pass at someone who was wearing a couples' shirt? That person was spoken for forever and was demonstrating it in the purest form – a shirt that looked exactly like their boyfriend or girlfriend. It was the obvious sign of true love!

You have already realized the obvious problem with these matching couples shirts – couples break up. When that occurred you had two choices: (1) throw the shirt away, or (2) hope your former "true love" did not wear their shirt on the same day you did!

Sunflower Seeds. In one of the elementary grades someone determined that the cool thing to do was to eat sunflower seeds. As soon as the word spread among my classmates, there was a "run "on the bags of sunflower seeds at Jarvey's. I am sure that in one week, Jarvey sold more bags of sunflower seeds than he had all year! But then the fad disappeared just a quickly as it came, leaving behind a lot of sunflower shells all over the place.

Sen-Sen. A quick "Google" of Sen-Sen reveals this important information: *"Sen-Sen was developed in the late 1800's by T.B. Dunn and Co., perfume dealers in Rochester, NY. According to Dunn's history, a plant supervisor by the name of Kerschner developed a formula for an effective and refreshing breath perfume. Sen-Sen are tiny pieces of licorice with a strong flavor that come in a red foil package. You only need a few of flakes to refresh your breath. Many would carry these envelopes in their pockets and pop a few in their mouth before a big date. Being they are in a foil envelope, they were easy to reseal for another time. At one time this anise flavored breath mints were America's most popular breath freshener."*

I am not sure which of my classmates was the first to eat sen-sen, but it caught on quickly. I bought one bag of these little black candies to see how they tasted, and was surprised that they simply tasted like black licorice. I concluded they were indeed a "breath mint" – if you wanted to have *bad* breath! I threw the rest of the bag away, and did not participate in the sen-sen fad again. Never liked licorice!

Large Dill Pickles. Although I never actually took part in this fad, I saw the girls in my class eating big dill pickles, at the Junior High basketball games. They must have bought them at the concession stand. They were individually wrapped and were approximately six inches long. I remember thinking that the girls in my class must really like dill pickles to eat such a big one!

Not knowing where to insert this true story about pickles, this looks like a good spot. My older sister, Pat, and I were sent on a mission one Thanksgiving Day. We were to go to the grocery store and buy a jar of pickles – but a very specific kind of pickles. They were to be Del Monte Kosher Dill Pickle Speers. We looked at every jar of pickles in the store, but none of them said exactly what we were told to buy. In desperation we did the only thing we knew to do – we tasted a few pickles to see which one was the right one.

The best-case scenario would have been to find the "right ones" on the first try, but unfortunately it took several tries before we found them. I have wondered all these years what the poor soul must have thought when they opened their newly purchased jar of pickles at home only to find that one of them had a big bite out of it!

Yes, you are probably right, that story may have been better left untold, for it does not speak well of what my mom used to call *"our raisin'"* (upbringing). Pat and I take full responsibility for that act, and realize now that it was not as funny as it seemed to be at the time.

Candy Buttons On Paper Rolls. Another Google search provides information about this fad candy of my childhood: *"Candy Buttons, Candy Dots, or Pox are small rounded pegs of candy that are attached to a strip of paper. This classic sugar candy was originally introduced by the Cumberland Valley Company. Necco acquired the brand in 1980, which made them the exclusive manufacturer of this product in the United States.*

Each strip of the candy includes three flavors: cherry (pink), lime (blue), and lemon (yellow). Candy Buttons come in two strip sizes - long and short. The long is 22½ inches, while the short is 11¼ inches. Necco makes 3/4 billion candy buttons in the course of a year."

In our chapter about Jarvey's Grocery Store, we mentioned that this was the candy of Jarvey's choice. He would make sure each kid that came by his counter got one of these "Jarvey pills" because, as he would say, "They are good for whatever ails you!"

Paraffin Bottles And Tubes of Flavored Liquids. The bottles or the tubes were about 5 inches long. One would bite off the paraffin end and drink the colored liquid inside. There were only a couple ounces of liquid inside, so it was not much of a "thirst-quencher." After the paraffin bottle or tube had been drained, it was optional as to whether you wanted to chew it up. Frankly, there was no taste to it at all. It was just like chewing paraffin, because it was.

I was surprised to learn on a recent trip to Cracker Barrel Restaurant that many of these old-time candies can still be purchased there.

These are not the only fads of the mid-50's and 60's, but

these were the ones I knew about or took part in. No doubt, there were dozens of other fads that existed but totally escaped my notice.

Chapter Twenty-One

The Old Baptist Church Hill

I refer to this hill as the "old" Baptist Church hill, because the Baptist Church of my youth was moved to an area on the south side of Carlisle next to Highway 5. In fact, the "new" Baptist Church was built in our back yard – actually a big pasture – in 1972.

The old Baptist church sat on the corner of N 3rd and Elm Street at the top of a hill. Looking north from the church, you could see what would later be developed as Echo Valley. If you traveled one block east of the church on Elm, you would have the option of turning north on N 2nd. This is where the real "fun" started.

Elm Street had an extremely steep downward grade, and once you turned north on N 2nd, the grade became even more severe. N 2nd went straight down for a quarter of a mile, then straight up for a quarter of a mile. This was a real challenge to a little boy in the mid-50's whose bike was a "one speed" (it only had one gear). You see, this was the shortest route to my grandma's house.

Two memories of the Baptist Church hill stand out in my mind, one is in the winter and the other is in the summer.

One Christmas vacation, we three kids took the new sleds we had been given for Christmas and headed off to find some good hills to slide down. Eventually, we wound up at the top of the hill by the Baptist Church. We had never slid down this hill before, because we had never had such aerodynamic, brand new sleds before, but now we were willing to try our luck.

We did not realize that the Baptist Church hill was not just covered with snow; the snow-covered street was covered with ice! Traffic may have worn away the ice had there been any traffic, but there had been none. The road was typical of what you would find in small town Iowa back then - not concrete, not blacktop; but hard packed gravel. Once every year or two, the road would be "oiled" in order to keep the dust down.

We ran, threw down our sleds, and hopped on one-after-the-other, so, all three of us were sledding down the Baptist Church hill at the same time. Maybe I should say we were "attempting" to slide down the Baptist Church hill at the same time. As we came to the corner where we were to turn left on N 2nd Street, we one-by-one catapulted into the air and into in the pasture about 20 feet from the road! I wouldn't want to tell you we were going fast, but I am absolutely sure we broke the land record for speed for a wooden sled that was only three weeks old!

No one was hurt, so we went to the top of the hill and tried it again. At the end of our sledding session, none of us had been able to make the turn at the corner of N 2nd and Elm Street. It was just too slick!

We then decided to start our slide partially down the hill, at the corner of 2nd and Elm. This worked well, and we went so fast that we almost made it up the other side of the hill!

None of us knew, that winter morning, that we were creating a memory that would be vivid in our minds 50 years later. That's the thing about memories - they never seem like memories at the time.

The other memory about the old Baptist Church hill has to do with going down the hill in the summer. Our usual policy was to walk our bikes down the first part of the hill, then at the corner of N 2nd Street, hop on and go as fast down the hill as we could. The faster we went downhill, the farther we went up the next hill, and the less hard pedaling we had to do.

One day I must have felt especially brave and decided to start at the top of the hill and ride all the way down. I rode the brake pretty hard until I came to the corner of N 2nd, turned and gave her the gas! I was going so fast, the pedals became useless. I could not pedal any faster than I was already going, so, I just held on! This would not have been as scary had the road been concrete or blacktop, but it was gravel! So, if you steered the front wheel too suddenly, you would certainly crash.

I told my brother and sister later that day that I must have hit at least 200 miles per hour, because I made it **all** the way up the hill without having to pedal even once! This was the only time this ever occurred in the Garnett family, before or after. No, I did not receive any award for this tremendous athletic feat, but it certainly was deserving of one. I never tried biking down that hill from the top again. After all, I had the coveted record. Why push your luck?

The Carlisle Missionary Baptist Church has been in existence for over 100 years, and for all the things it has been known for, to the Garnett kids, it was known for its hill!

Garnett Children Playing Peacefully At Tea Party (Rex Pegram's Yard In Background)
Circa 1955

Chapter Twenty-Two
I Know What I Don't Want To Be When I Grow Up

Our family was friends with a family that lived out on Scotch Ridge Road by the name of Van Ryswyk - Don, Rachel, and their three sons, Donnie, Dean, and Denny. Denny was a grade or two ahead of me in school, but we were still friends.

Our family used to go out to their house occasionally in the evening to "make music." Dad played the banjo, Mom the guitar, and all the adults would sing. We kids would listen for a few minutes, then play outside while the adults were doing their thing. Afterward there were refreshments, and that made it worth the trip.

I am not sure just how this took place, but one night it was decided that I would come back to their home the next day and spend the day on the farm. That sounded really exciting to a 10 year old "city boy." It was all new to me.

The next morning I was dropped off at their house to spend the day doing whatever farmers do on their farms. I did enjoy helping to gather eggs, feed the chickens, and give the cattle their hay. I even drove the tractor for a short distance, but did not score real high on that job experience, because I turned too sharp and hit a gate.

At lunch, Rachel served fried chicken, and she was a great cook! She also had one of the desserts she was famous for – chocolate cake.

Along toward the afternoon, Mr. Van Ryswyk and I were in a pen with a couple of calves. They seemed like big dogs to me, and I really enjoyed playing with them. I remember saying to Don, "You know, Don, this has been really neat. Maybe I will be a farmer when I grow up."

Just as the last word left my mouth, one of the little calves "let go" with a stream of poop like I had never seem before or have seen to this very day. It was similar to a "horizontal Old Faithful!"

Unfortunately, Don was standing directly behind the little calf when the geyser erupted and was instantly covered in calf poop from head to toe. I mean there was not a square inch of his body that was not saturated with that smelly goop!

Don looked up at me with a smile on his face and a twinkle in his eye and said, "Jimmy, are you still thinking about being a farmer when you grow up?"

I responded, "Nope - *anything but* a farmer!" It is funny how one brief experience can forever influence your thinking about a career. Never again did the thought of being a farmer enter my head! I still did not know what I wanted to be when I grew up, but I knew for sure what I didn't want to be!

Chapter Twenty-Three
Sunday Afternoon Football

We often enjoyed the same meal on Sunday noon – pot roast and potatoes with onion. Occasionally, my mom would throw in a couple of carrots, but I always thought they made the roast taste like cooked carrots. I realize that this was the goal, but I did not like cooked carrots and still don't!

In those days all the professional football games were played on Sunday afternoon – not Monday nights. They were also played outdoors regardless of how bad the weather was.

The football game came on just about the same time as we were sitting down to eat our pot roast lunch. People only had one TV back then, and it was located in the living room, so we usually took our TV trays into the living room and watched the game as we ate.

I do recall one Sunday pot-roast lunch that things did not turn out too well for our new cat. We had just purchased new carpet for the living room. It was a black and white sort of tweed look. My dad sat down in his chair with his tray on his lap to settle in and watch the game. Unfortunately, the new cat was not aware of the rule: "Do not jump on people's laps while they are holding a tray of food."

You guessed it – the cat jumped up in my dad's lap, dumping the entire plate of untouched roast, potatoes, and onion (no carrots) on the new carpet. I would not want to say my dad became angry, but I will tell you that this was the very first time I ever saw a cat fly. My dad grabbed it by the scruff of his neck, walked to the back door, and tossed it out into the yard. He would have won first place in the Olympic "cat throw." It was an amazing feat! I learned two things right then and there: (1) cats can fly, and (2) they do not *always* land on their feet. My sincere apologies to any cat lovers who are now angry with me for my lack of sympathy toward the new cat. After all, he should have known not to spill food on the new carpet.

There were great games to watch on Sunday afternoon. Our favorite was the Chicago Bears vs. the Green Bay Packers. The Bears were our favorite team with Mike Ditka, Dick Butkas, Jim Taylor, and Gale Sayers! The Packers were our least favorite team with players like Ray Nitschke, Paul Hornung, and Bart Starr.

If those two teams were playing each other, we would stay glued to the set until the final minute. But if the Sunday afternoon football game consisted of any other teams, a funny thing would occur. We would watch the first half, and as soon as it ended, we would head out to the high school football field. *Watching* football resulted in us having to *play* football, and it was so with many of our friends too. They would show up after halftime at the field.

By the time I hit the football field I was so pumped that

I just took off sprinting! I ran as fast as I could the full length of the football field, then I ran back again – and I was not the least bit winded or tired. I remember thinking one time that it seemed like I could run forever.

This memory, more than any other I have, makes me remember what it was like to be young. You never gave a thought as to what your body could or couldn't do. It worked flawlessly, and it did what you told it to do.

This memory, more than any other I have, also makes me realize what it is like to get older. I do have to consider what my 64 year-old body will or won't do. It no longer works flawlessly, nor does it do what I tell it to do. Now I have to be careful to walk that fine line between "warming up" and "wearing out!"

Sunday afternoon football. We watched it, we played it, we loved it! It was part of our youth growing up in Carlisle.

Chapter Twenty-Four
Two Trucks

Memories of my early childhood in Carlisle focus around two trucks. One was a milk truck and the other a pop truck.

The Milk Truck. Our milk used to be delivered right to our door when I was a little boy. Mom would give her order to the milkman, and he would put it in the metal "milk box" by the door. The milk came in glass bottles. He would normally come while I was still asleep.

Do you know how they kept the milk cold as they traveled on their routes all day long? Ice. There were no refrigerated trucks in the mid-50's because ice kept the milk cold. And back then, there was only one kind of milk you could order -white, 3.5 percent fat, whole milk. No chocolate. No skim. No, 2% of anything.

Sometimes when we would hear the milkman, we would run out to meet him. This was not because we knew him, but because we knew that there would be a possibility of him chipping off a piece of ice for each of us.

We would chew on the big piece of ice until our fingers got cold. Funny how excited we got over a piece of ice.

The Pop Truck. That is what we called it in my day – "pop." I never heard it referred to by any other name until we traveled out of Iowa to other sections of the country. We found out that some people called it "soda," while others (especially in the South) called it Coke. I guess it doesn't matter what you call it as long as the waitress understands what you want.

My dad bought his gasoline from the Conoco station up the road. It was owned by Harry Conant and sat at the intersection where School Street split off from Highway 5 and ran into Carlisle. It was a good location for a gas station.

We liked to go with Dad to get gas for two reasons. One reason was the gas pumps he used. The tops (domes) of the pumps were clear and had little balls in them that danced around when you were pumping gas. It was neat to watch them.

The other reason we liked to go to the gas station with Dad was the possibility of seeing the pop truck. I do not remember why, but on more than one occasion, the guy who delivered pop to Mr. Conant was unloading pop to his machines. He was also taking the cases of empty pop bottles with him and stacking them in a certain area on his truck.

 For some unknown reason, this pop man would take pity on the Garnett kids and give us a free bottle of pop. I doubt that our whining and unashamed asking had anything to do with it – he was probably just a Dad too, and liked making kids happy.

Most of the time the bottle of pop was warm, but that was ok with us. It came right off the truck, right out of the case where millions of other bottles of pop sat. After all, how many kids could say that they drank a bottle of pop right off the pop truck? Not many, I think.

I do not know why a free bottle of warm pop created a 55 year-old memory for me, but it has. Now that I think of it, it might be that there were not a lot of other competing events to rival the experience of "pop fresh off the pop truck" in Carlisle in the mid-50's.

Chapter Twenty-Five

Vacation Time

Every summer my dad thought it was very important for his family to take a vacation. There was no question as to where we would spend that vacation – with Mom's relatives in North Carolina. I think Dad felt he owed it to Mom to take her to see her family once a year. She was a young bride and came from a family of 12 kids! So, she had a lot of relatives to see, just in her immediate family alone.

So, just after school let out for the summer in late May, our family would plan to make the annual trip to see Grandma Horton and her three kids. Grandma mothered twelve children, and these last three were nearly the same age as we three kids. They were technically our uncles and aunts, but practically they were our cousins. This is especially true in light of the fact that they were certainly not any more mature or responsible than we were.

My dad's excitement about going on vacation was contagious. Just after the first of the year, while the snow was on the ground, he would order "travel maps" from "AAA Travel Club." These maps laid out a route from Carlisle, Iowa, to Mt. Airy, North Carolina. It never occurred to me at the time, but this was a bit unusual in that we went the same place every year. The need for maps to guide us when Dad could have driven there blindfolded was a bit unnecessary.

But I think the map service may have been free, and I think my dad asked them to take us through "new towns" along the route to Mt. Airy each year.

Sometime in late April or early May, the box of maps would arrive in the mail, and then the idea of going on vacation really began to sink in. Dad would get all the maps out of the box, put them in numerical order, lay them out on the floor, and begin to investigate the route that had been laid out for us for that year. I remember more than one night sitting on the floor with Dad as he outlined the route we were going to take. It was important to me because it was so important to him.

When Dad took a trip, he always referred to the familiar spots along the route like they were his old friends. For example, he would say, "Sally, they have us going down 'Old 54' again this year," or he might say, "We are going to be staying at the "Blue Haven" again in Mt. Carroll," or "Looks like we won't be going up "Big Walker Mountain until the second day." After I got a few trips "under my belt," I would have a mental image of these places and objects as he affectionately referred to them. You see, a vacation trip for my dad was much more than just a destination. He thoroughly enjoyed the journey to get him there, and his excitement and personal touch made vacation what it was to the Garnett family. It was kind of like Dad had a relationship with the trip itself.

It is hard to explain, but one thing is for sure – my dad created a lot of excitement about vacation just because of the things he did to personally prepare for it.

When the maps arrived, the three of us would be encouraged to start "saving our money for vacation." It would be pointed out to us that "You will want to buy souvenirs on vacation, and you'll need to have money for that." So, it was decided among the three of us that we would help each other save our money.

Each of us would find some sort of container to place our existing vacation money in, give it to the selected sibling, and they would "hide" it so we would not be tempted to spend it all before vacation came. If we wished to add to our existing "stash," we would give our money to "the guardian" and he would secretly get our container and add that amount to it. I vividly remember using a Davey Crockett powder pouch one year to hold my vast earnings. It was way cooler than what Howard or Pat put their money in!

I remember that we would try to get "the guardian" of our money to tell us where he had hidden it, but that information was a sacred thing, and never did we divulge the location. After all, what kind of a person would you be if you let your sibling go on vacation with no money? He would come home "empty handed" with no souvenirs, which of course would make one ask, "Why do you want souvenirs from the same place every year?" Go figure.

A few days before the departure date we got into the habit of doing something else. I must admit before I share this with you, that I am very aware *now* how weird this practice was, but it did not seem that way when I was seven or eight years old.

Well, here goes. A few days before the date we were to Leave, we would begin to write notes to our selves and go through a few rituals.

An average note would read something like this, "Dear Jim, I am writing this note on May 29th. When I get back from vacation, I am going to read this note and remember the time when I wrote this note."

We also had a birdhouse that was nailed about seven feet high on a wooden light pole that stood in our front yard. We would run fast, jump up and touch the birdhouse, and say, "I am going to remember this moment when I jumped up and touched this birdhouse when I get back from vacation."

My question to you would be, "What on earth do you think was wrong with us back then? Is that not about the weirdest thing you have ever heard?" Did you ever write yourself notes so you could read them later and remember the moment you wrote it? That is psycho.

Pat and I
In Our Front Yard
1953

To be honest with you, I think the purpose behind all that was to give us a perspective of how fast our vacation time would be over. It would seem like "just yesterday" that we had written the note or touched the birdhouse, and now vacation was over for another year! It was to create the old "tempest fugit" feeling – "time flies."

I can only say that as the youngest, I am sure that I did not think of those weird things to do! My suggestions were never considered seriously. The credit goes to my older brother and sister for whatever the three of us did. As the youngest, my suggestions were never considered seriously.

Now, on with the vacation saga (that was the weirdest part – it gets more normal from here on). On the night before we were to leave, we would get all of our clothes out and lay them on the bed to be packed. We did not actually put the suitcases in the trunk until departure time, so their presence in our bedroom only served to ramp up the excitement level to a fever pitch!

We took our baths and got to bed early. We needed to get our sleep so we could – do what – ride in the car for two days?

Dad would tell us, "Six o'clock is going to come awfully early. You kids be quiet now and get to sleep!" But who could sleep? We were in bed two hours earlier than normal, the car was parked on the grass near the front door, and our suitcases were screaming at us – "Close me up and let's get out of here!"

A few hours later Mom or Dad would awaken us and tell us it was time to go! Six o'clock had not come early! Six o'clock had not come at all, because it was only *two o'clock!* Dad could not sleep, so "we might as well leave a little early!" This happened year after year!

There would be very little talking as everyone hurried around doing his last minute things. The atmosphere seemed to be charged with excitement! The anticipation had been building since mid-April, and the time was here.

Each of us kids would sneak off to the secret place where we had hidden our sibling's vacation money, and we'd give it to its rightful owner (one year I hid my sister's money up in the bed springs of her bed). We would look inside the container to make sure it was all there, then give our monies to Mom so she could hold it for us until that special moment when we saw just the right souvenir!

Finally, suitcases would be packed in the trunk, a cooler of water would be placed on the floor of the back seat, a box of Kleenexes or a roll of paper towels would be laid on the shelf below the back window, a bag of fruit (apples to help you with – well, you know) would be set in the front seat floor, and the Garnett family would be headed out for their vacation for another year!

Two weeks later we would return home, weary from riding two days in the car, but happy to be back home. We would jump up and touch the birdhouse on the light pole and remember how we had pledged to remember doing that before we left, then we would find the note we had written to ourselves, read it, and throw it away (thinking that was stupid!).

Vacation had once again come and gone! The rest of the summer lay ahead of us. School was a long way off! Life was good. Everything was at peace. Carlisle was a good place to come back to!

Chapter Twenty-Six

The Night The Des Moines Police Department Almost Went To Jail!

When I was about eight years old, my dad starting coaching a men's slow pitch softball team. Dad was apparently quite a baseball player in his day, at least the articles about him when he played on a Navy team seemed to indicate that he was pretty exceptional third baseman.

The glove that my dad used was an "old-timey" glove. I actually could not believe someone could catch a ball with it, but when he wore it, he had no problem doing so.

One game, I think it was on the 4th of July, that Dad inserted himself into the lineup at 3rd base. Several times during the game he caught a hot grounder with his ungloved hand and whipped it to first in one fluid motion. I'm not sure how sore he was the next day, but it was obvious that he was quite a ballplayer. Even the young players on his team commented that he was certainly in a class above them.

When my dad took over the coaching responsibilities, those responsibilities took the form of a lot of little things that people would never consider. Dad would get to the diamond in the city park a couple of hours early so he could attach this chain link fence object to the back of the car and drag the diamond. Dragging it made it smooth so a ground ball would not hit a big dirt clod and jump up and hit the fielder in the face. I understood the level of his commitment the night he hooked up "the drag" to our brand new 1960 blue and white Nash Rambler and dragged the field before the game. Then he would line the field and turn the lights on.

He also led a campaign for the team to get uniforms, and solicited donations from the Carlisle businesses. The response was phenomenal and each new uniform had a Carlisle business sponsor logo on it.

Then he decided that there ought to be a permanent concession stand structure built, so whoever was playing at the time could sell pop, candy bars, and popcorn to help fund their team's expenses. I remember going with Mom to the diamond the afternoon of an evening game to stock the concession stand with pop and candy, and make sure it was ready to go for the evening. Mom often worked in it, but eventually most of the wives took their turns willingly.

The players not only became a good team on the field, they also became good friends off the field. Numerous times the players and their families would be invited to our home for pie and coffee. In the chapter where I write about the fireworks we bought for the 4th of July, I noted that several of the team players were at our house the night we were tossing cherry bombs and M-80's in our neighbor's yard. I am ashamed that we did that now, but at the time, it seemed quite the thing to do.

Howard Brown helped my dad coach while his son, Earl played shortstop (boy did he ever have an arm!). Vernie Thompson played third base and had the distinction of *always* having an opened bottle of Pepsi with him. During infield warm-ups, Vernie would set his bottle of Pepsi on the third base bag while he grounded the ball. I am sure the Government would have something to say about that today, but back then the Government paid more attention to its own business, than ours!

Norris Davis and Bob Underwood shared the catcher responsibilities, while Dick Patterson played second base. I just remembered as I was writing this article that Dad had a newspaper clipping of his old basketball town team and little Dick Patterson was sitting in the front row as their mascot. This was the Carlisle team that actually beat the nationally famous Globetrotters when they came to town!

Jim Turner played first base and occasionally caught, and Dick Hooper and Eddie Owens pitched. There were others like Jim and Bob Elmore, Richard Rothfus, Barnie Sneller, and others that played, but I can't recall their positions – not because I am old, but because I was young during the time they played!

The games for the most part were played for love of the game. There were occasional disputes, but no fights (except for the one I will tell you about in just a minute). Everybody took their turn in helping to do whatever needed to be done.

I believe it was my mom who served as the Carlisle Citizen newspaper liaison turning in the scores and commentary the day after each game. Some seasons we posted quite a few wins, and many of the citizens followed her reports each week.

The wives and families traveled to the away games, so it really was quite a crowd of people who took interest in the team. There were not so many competing interests for your attention in those days. It was similar to the days when the circus would come to town and everyone would go – after all, what else was there to do?

The game, by far, that was the most notable game my dad ever coached for the Carlisle men's softball team was the one played on the 4th of July around 1960. It was the evening game and drew a lot of interest because it was against the Des Moines Police Department, who had a good team.

Most of the people who were at the park for the 4th of July sauntered down to the field to watch as the game began. It proved to be as exciting as everyone had predicted. Both teams were playing well on offense and defense, and the score was very close.

Then their runner on 2nd base tried to make it all the way home on a hit to center field. Our center fielder made a great throw to Jim Turner, who was catching that night, and Jim was waiting for the runner as he neared home plate.

Their runner apparently had never had any lessons in how to slide into a base, so he chose to put his head down and simply ran full speed into our catcher. Had there been the ability to call an "unsportsmanlike conduct" call, which would have merited one! Running into another player like that was totally uncalled for.

I was sitting in the stands between third base and home plate, so I had a pretty good view. It all happened very fast. I remember seeing our catcher fly into the air and land somewhere near the backstop. The impact had made him drop the ball so the runner was safe. Instead of helping our catcher up, he said something to Jim that was not nice. Jim came up off the ground and grabbed their runner by the neck, and they began to wrestle.

Boy, did that set things into motion! Before you could say "You're safe," players from both teams emptied their dugouts and ran onto the field pushing and shoving each other. For over ten minutes, no one could tell the difference between law-enforcement officials and average citizens. Remember, their players were Des Moines Policeman.

I was sitting near Bogey Turner, the catcher's Dad. I am not sure at which moment Bogey left his seat, but he was down the bleachers and on the field in a flash. It made absolutely no difference to him that these opposing players were policemen, "Nobody runs into my son like that!" Boogie had to be in his sixties and was our high school janitor. He also had apparently taken some boxing lessons along the way, because he was right in there duking it out with the cops!

Eventually, our town policeman, Dale Prall, entered the playing field. Dale was a large man and not hard to see, especially if he wanted to be seen. He was also not hard to hear. I remember hearing him say to their coach, who I found out later was a police captain, "I don't care if you are cops – if you don't settle down, you are all going to jail!" That's the way to tell 'em, Dale!

I ask you, "Is that excitement or what?" What an ending to the 4th of July in Carlisle! The game was called a draw and was stopped with that play. I don't think it would have been safe to try another inning, or even another play.

The front-page headline on the Des Moines Register the next morning read, "Police Threatened With Jail In Goodwill Game." Whoever reported that story had apparently attended the game and certainly had all the facts. There were quotes from just about everyone, including my dad, and radio interviews with the players and coaches and fans. Let's face it, it was not good publicity for the Des Moines Police Department. It would have made absolutely no difference if the runner's action was fair or unfair, the policemen coming to a small town celebration and fighting was frowned on by the public. It was not a good day to be a Des Moines cop. They looked pretty silly.

We were amazed at the play the story about the game received. For weeks afterward, people from across America sent us newspaper clippings about the game. We even received a copy of "The Stars and Stripes" newspaper from the Philippines where it
made the headlines.

I do not want to say whether that 4th of July softball game (and fight) was my dad's legacy or not, but there was nothing he ever did, before or afterward, that got such far reaching coverage or attention!

So, now you know "the rest of the story." Forty years before Carlisle was known as the city of the septuplets, it was known "as the city where the Des Moines police department almost went to jail!" Yep, that was my dad's team all right, and we three kids were proud of it!

The Carlisle slow-pitch, men's softball team - my dad's team! Those times serve to be some of the fondest memories I have of being a kid growing up in Carlisle.

Dad died in December, 2001. He was a great baseball player, a great coach, and a great dad. I miss him.

Howard, Dad, and Myself
At the Carlisle Park, July 4, 1960

Chapter Twenty-Seven

My Experiences With The Evils of Tobacco

I have three vivid memories of dealing with the evils of tobacco while growing up. Before I share these, let me remind you that in that era, smoking was not considered bad for your health. In fact, it seemed like everybody smoked, especially everybody on TV. Most people did not consider using tobacco a good habit, but it was not frowned upon nearly as much as it is today.

My first experience with tobacco took place while we were vacationing at my grandma Horton's house in North Carolina, when I was around 5 years old. Someone said it would be a good idea to visit Grandpa and Grandma Weddle who lived at the top of a very winding rode on a very big mountain somewhere in North Carolina.

Grandpa Weddle, whose first name was "Hasting," grew his own tobacco and carried a "plug" of it with him in his pocket. This plug resembled a Baby Ruth candy bar.

Hasting and Sarah Weddle

I remember watching him cut off "a chew" as he rocked on the porch of his tin roofed home. I politely asked him if I could have some of that stuff too? He smiled at me as he cut me off a 2-inch section of his homegrown tobacco plug, and told me to stick it in my jaw. He said, "Be sure you don't chew it."

I wish now that he would have also said, "Be sure you don't chew it *or swallow the juice*," but he omitted that last important information. So, I did what I was told – I did not chew on the tobacco, *but I did swallow the juice*!

The physical reaction was somewhere between having an out-of-body hallucination and contracting rabies! I began to sweat, became dizzy and nauseated, and eventually vomited. Believe it or not, if I close my eyes and think back about that awful experience, I begin to get nauseated!

I have always wondered if Grandpa Weddle purposely did that to me to make me avoid chewing tobacco? I do remember that he did not seem to be overly alarmed that I got sick from the piece he gave me.

My second experience with tobacco also took place in North Carolina at my grandma Horton's house –maybe I should say her "outhouse." Uncle Junior and my brother Howard were 4 years older than I was, so I tagged along with them most of the time.

One day I noticed they went into Grandma's outhouse together, so I followed them, knocked on the door, and said "Let me in."

Once in, I saw that they had confiscated a pack of cigarettes and were lighting them up and smoking them one after the other. When the cigarettes became short, they threw them down one of the two holes (yes, Grandma's outhouse was a two-seater).

After I had taken a couple of puffs, I heard girls laughing and could see (through the opening in the wall boards) my sister Pat and my aunt Wanda running up the hill. It was through that very same crack in the wall that I saw my dad coming down the hill just a few minutes later!

He knocked on the door of the old outhouse and said, "What are you boys doing in there?" Now, my dad was not blind, and he could clearly see the smoke coming out of all the holes in the outhouse walls. He knew what we were doing.

Dad asked, "Are you boys smoking?" and we replied, "No, we are not smoking." Then we reluctantly unlatched the outhouse door and watched the smoke billow out like smoke signals sent by an Indian tribe.

Then, one by one he made us pass by him and blow into his face so he could smell our breath. We ran to the house crying (so as to not incur further punishment) but soon met the fate of getting a spanking. Dad said the spanking was not for smoking, but for lying to him.

I didn't quite understand all that, but since Dad smoked cigarettes like a locomotive, the lying angle sort of made sense.

After 60 years, my brother and I remember that experience as though it happened yesterday. And just for the record, we do NOT hold a grudge toward our sister for tattling. The snitch.

My third and last experience with tobacco occurred while I was in fifth grade. I had spent the night with Steve Haltom on a Friday night. I recall getting up early the next morning because Steve had a paper route to deliver.

His mother, Darlene, was in the bathroom getting ready as we left, but after going out the door, Steve told me to wait in the driveway, and he went back inside.

I was a bit surprised to find when he joined me that he had gotten into the hall closet and had taken a pack of his mom's cigarettes! If I remember correctly, the pack was empty when we came home later that morning. I am guessing that there must have been 20-25 cigarettes in that pack, and we smoked every one of them!

Here is the interesting part of this story. When we arrived back home, his mom had left for work, but on the brick steps leading up into the house were two very carefully placed cigarettes!

No one ever said a word to us about what we had done, but we got the uncanny feeling that we had fooled no one! She knew exactly what had taken place!

From that day on, I began to notice my parents were actually a lot smarter than what I previously thought. Like Darlene, they seemed to know what I was doing most of the time, even when I tried to fool them.

I have often thought of Steve's mom's action of laying those cigarettes on the steps. You know, that was simply brilliant!

Chapter Twenty-Eight

Rub-A-Dub-Dub, Three Kids In A Tub

To tell you the truth, this particular memory is pretty vague. Seeing pictures of the event stirs faint recollections of it actually happening.

I'm talking about those times when at a very early age (I mean still in diapers), the Garnett children went "skinny dipping" in their own front yard. Although the Carlisle Citizen never made a headline story out of it, it was a big enough happening that someone at our house took pictures!

My mom had a wringer washer, which consisted of the main tub that housed the agitator and the wringer that sat above the tub. Then to the side of the main tub would be two big washtubs.

The clothes went in the main tub filled with soapy

water, then were wrung out once or twice in the wringer, then dipped in the two tubs of rinse water and wrung out again. If this didn't get them clean and/or rinsed well enough, the process started over again. This procedure was actually considered somewhat of a modern appliance. It was a definite improvement over its predecessor, the washboard.

 Mom would take the two grey washtubs, plus another big, oval, copper tub and set the three of them in a row under the big elm tree which sat about 40 feet from the front door. I refer to this door as our "front door" because

that is how everybody entered our house, but it was actually not the door that faced the street. Only strangers came to that door. It was on the east side of our house.

She would then put water in each tub from the garden hose and add warm water from the house. Then we took off all our clothes and got in the tubs.

I think the pictures I saw had me sitting in the oval copper tub. I thought at first that I must have chosen that one, and then I realized that, as the youngest, I did not get first choice on anything. On second thought I realized that the copper oval tub was the narrowest of the three tubs and being the smallest, I fit into it better than anyone else.

As I mentioned, I only have faint memories of being involved in the activity, so I do not have any stories to tell about it. The reason I mention it is that I thought it might possibly stir up some of your old memories about "bathing" in your mom's washtubs in your front yard when you were a kid.

It might seem strange to today's parents to put your kids in washtubs to play on a hot summer's day, but considering there was no air conditioning back then, it was a smart way to make the kids happy and get some cute pictures! Those of you who were "tubbers" will agree that these are the kind of pictures that you pray never surface to the light of day!

Chapter Twenty-Nine

Cousin Susie

I have a good friend who lives in Carlisle. You may know her as Susan Robinson, but I know her as Susie Randleman, or better yet "Cousin Susie." We have been friends for almost as long as we have been cousins – over 60 years!

My grandma, Mabel Randleman-Garnett, and Susie's Grandpa Fred Randleman were brother and sister. They were both children of Hix and Ellen Randleman, whose house sits on 245 Pennsylvania Street in Carlisle. This house was built in 1907, and my grandma Mabel moved into it with her family when she was around 16 years old.

This grand house must have been a sight to behold in its day. Even 100 years later, its ornate carvings and elaborate décor are breathtaking. If you have not visited the Randleman House, you really ought to; it is quite an exquisite historical treasure for the town of Carlisle.

Top: 1907 picture of the Randleman house during construction.

Right: The elaborate woodwork above the entrances into the ground floor rooms

My dad, Lyle Garnett, spent a lot of time in the Randleman House in his early years, since his Grandma Ellen babysat for him during the day while his mom and dad were running their grocery story in downtown Carlisle.

I recently visited the Randlehouse with Cousin Susie and stood in the upstair's room that had been my grandma's bedroom. Looking out her large window, I gazed upon the big oak tree that stood near the house and wondered if my dad has ever tried to climb it. It was a really nostalgic moment that made me feel close to my grandma and to my dad.

Back to Susie Randleman. Sometimes we walked to or from school together when we were little. It was really nice to have a girl cousin in the same grade as I. It allowed both of us to have a friend of the opposite sex that we could talk to and hang around without being seen as boyfriend and girlfriend.

We were in the "afternoon" kindergarten class together as you can see below. It was apparently Christmas time since the boys are wearing Santa suits. You can see that Cousin Susie sported long braids when she was little. I took a special interest in them.

If you could clearly see my face in this picture, I look like I am about ready to do something I shouldn't, which would not be a stretch of anyone's imagination.

You can also see a glimpse of the shelving directly behind the kids in this picture. These compartments stored our mats for "nap time." I have to tried to preserve the practice of "nap time," but I no longer use a mat.

On with my story. In our classroom, Susie's desk was in front of mine. I tried hard to pay attention to Mrs. Wilson, but it was difficult with Susie's long braids dangling right in front of my face. I could almost hear them calling to me "Pull me! Pull me!" They were right there within my reach! Who could blame me for grabbing one of them and giving it a good yank?

So, I did what any little six-year-old boy would do – I reached up and grabbed one of them, and gave it a yank! I will forever remember Susie's reaction – she spun around without saying a word, took her pencil (that was supposed to be used "only for writing") and poked me in the leg!

I don't remember her making a noise when I yanked her braid, but I do remember saying "Ouch!" when she stuck me with her pencil. That drew the teacher's attention, and I was in trouble. Even before she asked, the teacher knew that Susie had not instigated the problem. My past had sold me out once again!

After that incident, I saw things as a definite draw - no winner and no loser. She got "yanked" and I got "stuck," everybody was equal. There was no reason to continue the warfare. It was time to lay down our weapons and declare peace.

Fast forward to our senior year of high school. I served as Student Council President, a job that unfortunately took me out of the classroom on numerous occasions. There was always some pressing "Student Council business" that demanded my time and attention.

Susie was nominated for Homecoming Queen along with four other deserving candidates: Celeste Stephens, Lee Hakes, Juanita Peno, and Valerie Mills.

I remember well the evening that all the queen candidates were seated on the stage in the old gymnasium, waiting for the announcement to be made by the Student Council President as to who would be crowned the 1967 Homecoming Queen

I had decided to walk behind each seated candidate, out of her line of vision, so I could approach the winner from behind and set the crown on her head. Of course, I knew Susie had won, but I walked behind each candidate and paused so as to create some excitement. It seemed a better option than just reading the winning name at the first.

I paused behind Susie's chair, making the crowd wonder if she was the winner. I then approached her and set the crown down on her head. But after setting the crown on her head, I lifted it slightly, giving the impression I was going to remove it. I was trying to add some excitement to the moment, but when everyone gasped especially Susie, I put the crown back down on her head right away and left it there! I knew immediately that the "up and down" thing was a mistake, but the deed was already done. This picture from the high school annual of 1968 shows me setting the crown on Susie's head. I am not sure if this was the first time or the second that I set the crown on her head.

Frankly, the thing I have wondered about to this very day is why cousin Susie has never retaliated to my stupid up and down crown trick!" Yes, I apologized to her afterward, but it would certainly not have surprised me if there still had been some sort of a "payback" down the road. I deserved a payback when I yanked her braid in kindergarten class, and I deserved a payback for the "bouncing crown" trick, but nothing ever happened afterward.

 This picture shows me leading Queen Susie to her throne, while her escort, Jack Shoop (her boyfriend at the time) can be seen in the background.

My obvious concern in sharing this story with you is that I now is reminded Cousin Susie about this incident. Maybe she will plan some horrible retaliation against me! After all, she has had 50 years to think up some kind of payback! It is simply frightening!

So, let it be known to all citizens of Carlisle and the surrounding area - if I disappear from off the face of the earth, Susie Randleman-Robinson should be regarded as the #1 suspect and should be questioned immediately!

Lee Hakes and Mark Ewers riding with the 1962 Homecoming Queen Joyce Hughes.

Chapter Thirty

Going Solo

When I was ten years old, I went to the barbershop by myself for the first time. Mom had given me the money to pay for my haircut, and I had it tucked securely in my pocket.

The barbershop was located in downtown Carlisle and was owned by an older gentleman who had barbered in Carlisle for many years. His son had recently come to work for him, so at that time, Carlisle had two barber chairs going at the same time – quite a phenomenon for our fair city, we thought.

The older fellow had cut my hair previously, but I much preferred the way his son cut it. His son listened to how I wanted it cut, while the older gentleman pretty much cut it the way he wanted.

The barbershop was packed that day, and I did not know for sure who was ahead of me. I was hoping that it would just work out that my turn would have me going to the son's chair, not the older guy's. But as the older barber finished his customer, he looked at me and said, "You're next."

Oh, no! Now what was I going to do? I did not want him to cut my hair. I wanted his son to do it. I had seen other people ask for his son, but I was not sure how to ask for him.

So, I said as nonchalantly as I could, "I want to wait for the other guy." He gave me a surprised look and said, "What did you say?" So I said matter-of-factly, "I want to wait for the other guy."

 My request seemed to irritate the older barber, and he said to me abruptly, "Don't you think I know how to cut hair?" I wasn't sure why he was so upset, but I responded as truthfully as a 10 year-old

little boy could, "Yes, sir, I know you can cut hair. You have cut my hair before." But then to explain my reasoning, I added, "But he cuts my hair better than you do!"

That really set him off! I was not trying to be smart, but that *was* the reason I wanted his son to cut my hair. It wasn't because I liked the color of his chair better – he cut my hair better! I didn't understand why this was a problem.

But it was a problem – for him! He barked out in a loud voice, "You either get in my chair right now, or you will go to the end of the line."

Everyone in the room was silent, even his son, who didn't raise his head. It was really embarrassing, and I did not know what to do. So, I did what my instincts told me to do. I went to the coat rack, grabbed my coat, and went out the door without saying a word.

As I walked home, I thought over what had happened. I did not think I had done anything wrong, and I wasn't sure why my request had bothered the older guy so much. After all, if I were going to pay for it, couldn't I have my hair cut by anyone I wanted?

I also wondered, as I walked home, whether anyone in the barbershop had spoken up in my defense after I left? After all, I was only a dumb kid wanting to get a hair cut. Maybe one of those adults should have said to the older barber, "Why don't you just relax and let the kid get his hair in whichever chair he wants? You still get paid for it anyway."

I knew my dad would never have tolerated him bullying me like that. I saw Dad go to my brother's defense once when one of the school coaches said something to Howard that was rude and inappropriate. After my brother shared the incident with Dad, Dad said he was going down to the school and "talk to that guy!" We knew that "that guy" was a big dude – much bigger and much younger than my dad. So, we told Dad as he went out the door, "Be careful, he is a really big guy!" to which my dad responded, "He may get a meal, but I'll get a sandwich!"

That was the first and last time I ever heard that expression. I am sure it originated from Dad's Navy's days, but it expressed my dad's vigor to stick up for his kids when he felt they had been treated unjustly.

Of course, my folks noticed that I did not have any shorter hair than when I left, so I explained to them what had taken place. They asked me several times if I had been disrespectful to the barber, and I told them I did not think I had. I was a bit scared when he barked at me, and my voice was kind of shaky, but I don't think anyone there would say that I was disrespectful to him.

My dad told me that I had a right to choose who cut my hair, and the man had been wrong in taking offense at that. He also told me that he was proud of me for standing up for myself without being a smart aleck.

I forgot about the matter for several weeks, but by that time, my hair really needed to be cut. I had no option – there was only one barber in Carlisle! My mom offered to cut it, but I remembered the haircuts she used to give where the clippers "yanked" out more hair than they cut. So, I went back to the same barbershop with my money tucked in my pocket. I went back with fear and trembling.

I tried to figure out with the number of people ahead of me, how the rotation would work out. Fortunately for me, the son's chair became empty at just the right time and he looked at me and smiled and said, "You're next."

I never brought up the subject and neither did he. He just cut my hair *the way I wanted it cut* and that was that. Shortly thereafter, the older barber's son left the barbershop, and a new barbershop opened up just a block away. I went to the new one until I left Carlisle after graduation.

I am sure you want to know what lessons I learned through all this at age 10? Frankly, I am not sure I learned any profound lessons at the time – I was only 10 and was not particularly focused on learning life-lessons.

But if someone would have asked me at that time, "How did you like going to the barbershop alone for the first time?" I think I would have responded, "It was good to feel grown up, but going with my dad still has some real positive advantages!"

Isn't that a problem we all faced as we grew up? Embracing the freedoms of "going it alone," meant we had to leave behind some of the "safety" that being a kid provided. Thus, we learn that growing up has its advantages and its disadvantages.

Dad And I At The Carlisle Home
Circa 1998

Chapter Thirty-One
Basement Basketball

One of the things that my grandpa and grandma's house had that our house did not have was a basement. It also had a standup attic where some really neat things were stored, like the old time windup Victrola and a Beaver stovetop hat. But let's concentrate on their basement.

It is somewhat amazing to me that I remember so much about their basement. I never set out to remember anything about it, and actually did not pay much attention to my surroundings down there at the time. But when I stop and reflect on it, a lot of details come to mind.

When you entered Grandpa and Grandma's house from their back door next to the garage, you immediately had the choice of going up the stairs to the left and into the kitchen, or down the stairs to the right into the basement.

As you reached the bottom of the stairs, you found

yourself in a large rectangular room with an unpainted concrete floor and painted block walls. As I look back, I am guessing this room must have been fifty feet long and thirty feet wide.

To the left of this bigger room were two smaller rooms. The first room was the coal room, where the coal-burning furnace sat with a large pile of coal in front of it. On the wall were hung several small shovels, one a red handled shovel that I believe my brother still has today.

I never thought about it then, but I know now that the coal was dropped into this room through a coal chute (a little door that opened to the outside just to the left of the back door). The pile of coal in the room must have been fifteen feet by fifteen feet and about 3-4 feet tall. It never occurred to me then, but I realize now that Grandpa would have to go into that room frequently and shovel coal into his furnace to heat his house.

If you walked through the coal room, you exited into another small room that was grandpa's workroom. Grandpa was a carpenter, and this room was filled with his tools. It was also filled with coffee cans full of "mysterious items" that lined a half dozen shelves that sat above and around his workbench.

Grandpa also was a painter and paperhanger, thus this room smelled like turpentine from cleaning his brushes. Lying on the workbench and hanging on carefully placed nails were his paintbrushes and his paper hanging tools.

The thing that always caught my attention was the wheel that was screwed into the workbench. It had a handle on it that was just waiting to be turned by a little boy. And turn it I did! Round and round till I could turn it no faster, and then I would release the handle and watch it spin till it stopped. Then I would do it again. Sometimes we would see who could make it spin the longest. On the right wall of the workroom was a door that brought you back into the large room you entered at the bottom of the basement stairs.

As you faced the basement stairs, you noticed a large sunken floor drain in the middle of the room on the right side. I think this is where grandpa actually cleaned his paintbrushes, because it smelled like turpentine too. This is also where my brother and I chose to go to the bathroom instead of running all the way up the stairs to use the facilities that were created for this purpose. This, of course, has been a family secret hidden from our family members until now.

Occasionally, we would go into the coal room or the workroom, but primarily we would play in the large room. One game that we played above and beyond all others was basketball. This game was not played with a real basketball, but with a basketball made out of an old pair of socks with a rubber band around them. At times we resorted to wadding up newspaper into a ball if there were no socks available.

Our basketball hoops were made from coat hangers that we had fashioned into circular hoops. Those hoops seemed to be really high at that time, but in reality they could not have been over seven foot tall!

One could not "bounce" the ball, because the ball, you recall, was a wadded up pair of old sox. Thus, you were allowed to take only a couple of steps and then you had to shoot. The defending player often assumed the role of Wilt Chamberlain as he stood in front of the hanger (oops, I mean hoop) and jumped up to block the shot.

It was a far cry from an "indoor gym," but it served our purpose.

Pat, Granma, Mom, Howard
Circa 1947

One of the last times we played basketball in Grandpa and Grandma's basement, we had grown to the point where you could stand flat-footed and block shots that were going into the hoops. That was not real fun, so we pretty much called it a good run and hung up our socks, I mean our basketball.

Some of the lights in the basement turned off and on from a switch at the top of the stairs. But other basement lights turned off with a pull string. More than once I was sent to a light that needed to be turned off with a pull string, and as I pulled the light off, I realized my brother and sister were at the top of the stairs waiting. When my light went off, they switched off the switch and there I was in a totally dark basement scared half to death!

After years of therapy, I have forgiven my brother and sister, and am making progress on stopping the nightmares that haunted me at night.

I was advised to think of grandpa and grandma's basement in a positive way. In fact, that is why I wrote this chapter on "basement basketball." Remembering it that way has had a soothing effect on me instead of remembering it as the place where I was scared out of my wits!

Chapter Thirty-Two

Laying "Leather"

If you were to tell me about the dumbest thing you ever did, does anything come to mind? Or maybe rather than try to decide on one thing, your mind is flooded with numerous things that would compete for first place?

One of the dumbest things I ever did, I did when I lived in Carlisle as a young lad. You know by now that I grew up with an older sister, Pat, and an older brother, Howard. They were three and four years older than me, so you can guess who got the worst of almost every situation in our home! To my advantage, though, Mom did a pretty good job of equalizing the sides!

Although I never told my older brother, he was always kind of a hero to me. He was just so darn cool that I couldn't help but want to be like him. He was smart, athletic, and seemed to be able to date really pretty girls. Following behind him in school was neat because all the teachers liked him (in

151

other words he was a kiss up). Therefore, they liked me even before they met me. I was "Howard Garnett's brother" to them. The basketball coach, Dwight Subbert, even thought I would have some of my brother's basketball ability – boy did he get a shock! It only took one practice to change his expectations!

Howard and his friends were never unkind to me, so to speak, but that is only because I was virtually invisible to them. I was just a fat little kid with nothing to add to their vast, worldwide experiences, so I was pretty much ignored.

One day my big brother was talking with his friends in a little group over by themselves. I remember some of the guys in that group – Dave Baber, Larry Crook, Jon Black, and others I can't recall. As luck would have it, I saw an opportunity to make myself "visible" in their sight. It was an opportunity handed to me on a silver platter.

Car "Laying Rubber"

An older student with a cool car had stopped at the stop sign not far from where we were all standing, and when he pulled out from his stop, he decided to show off for the girls and "gun it." When he stepped on the gas his tires squealed, and he left black tire marks on the pavement. We called that "peeling out."

I glanced over to Howard's group to see their reaction, but they had not seen it nor heard it. Here was my chance – I saw something really neat that none of them had witnessed. I had information – important information – to share with them that would elevate me in their eyes.

I ran over to the group and without waiting for a pause in their conversation, I blurted out, "Hey guys (like I was one of the guys), did you just see Darryl lay leather?"

Now, for those of you who do not realize the "faux pas" (social blunder) I had just committed, I will tell you. The other phrase we used to describe "peeling out" was "laying **rubber**," obviously because those black tire marks left on the road are the result of the **rubber** tires spinning and leaving **rubber** on the road.

Laying **rubber** – that was the phrase I had wanted to use, but instead I said, "Darryl laid LEATHER!" Let me tell you, my attempt at trying to ease my way into their social status was just set back at least 100 years! There was nothing that had ever occurred in history that was referred to as "laying *leather*," yet that is what I said! It made absolutely no sense!

Howard's group just stood there for a moment as if they had been touched with a stun gun. No one said a word. Then it must have come to them all at the same time - what I was trying to convey was that someone had just laid *rubber*. They starting laughing. I mean I thought some of them were going to need CPR because they laughed so hard they could not get their breath!

All of them laughed at me, except my brother Howard. He just looked at me as though he was beyond belief that I could ever say anything so stupid.

So, with his friends still laughing, and Howard still looking, I just walked away without another word.

I could not have been over 10 years old, and yet had already been exposed to what it was like to make a total, absolute, complete fool of myself. I said "Darryl laid *leather*," not "Darryl laid *rubber*," and I remember how I felt to this day. I could not have looked more like an idiot had I tried.

What did I learn? I learned to give my big brother space, and not try to impress his friends. The cost was way too high, because with only one misplaced word I could forever label myself as an un-cool, uninformed, uneducated twit.

I guess the most amazing part of this whole story is that my brother has never brought up that incident to me. Just think of how he could have used that as an "ace in the hole" against me for years – yet he never brought it up! I am not so sure I would have been so gracious to him.

"Darryl laid *leather*" – Geez - I still cannot believe I said that!

Chapter Thirty-Three

A Lesson From Grandpa Fred

Early Picture of
Grandpa Fred

It was Thanksgiving time and Mom had cooked her traditional turkey, mashed potatoes, dressing, and pumpkin pie. Every year I would try to like the cranberries, but every year they tasted just like they did the year before! They were and are still not for me!

I had just gotten my driver's license, so I volunteered to go get

Grandpa Fred across town. It was another excuse to drive. I am so glad I did, because almost 60 years later, I still remember the lesson he taught me that day.

Grandma Mabel has passed away a couple of years before, and Grandpa was living by himself. We all loved having him come over to our house, and he seemed to enjoy it as well.

I pulled into his driveway, turned off the 1960 Nash Rambler (which my dad had purchased brand new – and which the horn honked every time we turned a corner after driving it out of the car lot, so we turned around and took it back!).

Grandpa Fred had his coat on and was sitting in the kitchen waiting for me. He had bought a couple packs of rolls to contribute to the meal, so he grabbed them and we were out the door.

Just as we reached the car, a bird decided to "make a deposit" on Grandpa Fred's shoulder. He mumbled something about the bird, took out his ever-present handkerchief and wiped off the residue from his coat. On the way to the house I brought up the mathematical possibility of that bird flying over at just the right time and dropping his deposit at just the right angle to hit Grandpa's shoulder. I thought it was an amazing feat! Grandpa, on the other hand, did not seem too impressed by it.

We joked again about it one more time, and by then, were pulling up in our driveway. I got out of the car and went around, opened his door, and asked if he needed any help in getting out. He grabbed his two packs of rolls and started into the house, but he hadn't taken five steps before a bird decided to "make another deposit" on him – this time, on his head!

Can you imagine that? What would the mathematical possibility be of that happening twice to the same person in one day? I have read that the odds are one in a billion that a bird will poop on you once. This was now the second time to the same person, same day!

As I saw the white deposit hit the top of his head, I dropped to my knees laughing! I had never seen anything so funny in all my life!

I have since become aware of the fact that many people view a bird pooping on you as a stroke of "good luck." They say that the odds are so small, that if a bird poops on you, you could probably win the lottery too! I have to say, that is some strange reasoning! Grandpa Fred certainly did not see it as his "lucky day."

He took out handkerchief again, carefully manipulated it so he wouldn't use the same spot as he had previously, and wiped it off.

Then he looked at me with a twinkle in his eye and said, "Jimmy, some days it just doesn't pay to get out of bed!"

That comment did not equate to any profound life-lesson for me at that time, but as the years have gone by I have, for some reason, remembered that day.

Forrest Gump's mom was correct when she said to him, "Life is like a box of chocolates – you never know what you're gonna' to get." Some days give you pleasure and some days give you pain – and *some days the bird will poop on you, not only once, but twice!*

Just wipe it off the best you can and go on! Tomorrow will be another day, and the birds may all be grounded.

Chapter Thirty-Four
Best Friends

When I think back to my childhood days, many of my memories include Gary Rothfus. I guess you could say we were best friends for a really long time, through elementary school, through college, and to the present day. I am not sure just what cemented our friendship together, other than the fact that Gary always wanted to be like me. I knew that would get your attention, but it isn't true.

Some of our first contacts came from attending the Avon Church together. I remember on one of my first visits to the church, Gary invited me to a picnic the church was hosting that afternoon. From there on, we just sort of hit it off. We had similar interests and similar abilities so that probably helped.

Gary lived on a farm west of Carlisle, and I lived in town. That made for pretty interesting visits to each other's homes, especially when I got to ride the school bus to his house after school. I thought that was really neat, but since he did it every day, it was no big deal to him.

On one overnight stay at his house, we had a spectacular pillow fight that even included his older brother, Don. I know we got in big trouble with Gary's mom, Frances, but I am not sure why. My memory recalls something about a broken window, but the details are too fuzzy to put together.

Gary and I went to the Iowa State Fair together one year. He was really into playing arcade games, so we spent a lot of time in the arcade tent. We decided to take a walk through the midway (carnival) area. We were told the same thing about the people who ran the midway as those who ran the carnival at the Carlisle 4th of July – they were gypsies who might steal you away if given the chance. So, we both kept a sharp eye on them.

I remember we stopped at one game to try to figure out just what you were supposed to do to win. It had something to do with throwing balls at dolls. Finally, in desperation I said to the man running the game, "Hey, mister, how do you play this game?" His response was a sharp rebuke: "The more you knock down the more you win, Gourd Head!" Apparently, he was convinced there was little money to be earned from a couple of ten year olds. He had no time for our silly questions, and no reason to be polite!

That was the very first time either of us had ever heard someone called a "gourd head," and it really struck us funny. We both dropped to our knees, laughing so hard we didn't make a sound! I believe that response made the game host even more upset with us, and he mumbled something that I know could not have been nice. I think he thought we were laughing at him, which was partially true, but basically at what he had said to us.

We finally managed to get back on our feet and journey on down the midway, but for weeks we would look at each other and say "gourd head," and then break into laughter. In fact, I am absolutely sure that if I talked to Gary today, some 55 years later, and said "gourd head," he would laugh and know exactly what I was talking about!

Here's a picture I just found in my picture pile from sixth or seventh grade. Gary wrote on the back: *"Dear Jim, You are a friend so true , but I'm sure glad I don't look like you (cause you're ugly). I didn't mean what I wrote – you really look like a fat, old goat! From Gary."*

Now doesn't it just warm your heart to read those endearing words from one friend to another?

I also noticed as I went through my pile of old pictures, that I must have been short on friends that particular year. I have over a dozen of that year's pictures left, meaning I did not give them away to anyone! That's one of the worst things that can happen to you – a left over stack of class pictures!

I recall two incidents involving Gary that had to do with cars. One was the summer job we had of mowing the Avon Cemetery that was out in the country. It was a big cemetery and had several oval roads in it. We, of course, referred to these oval roads as "race tracks."

During our lunch breaks, we would do time trials on the tracks, with me driving my 1954 Ford (that I bought for $50), and Gary driving his farm pickup that had a windshield you could prop open and an absent radiator cap. I know this because while driving his pickup on a time trial, I hit a big bump and hot radiator fluid sloshed through the open windshield and burned me!

The other incident involving a car had to do with Gary's 1960 white Rambler. This was Gary's first time to drive because he had just gotten his driver's license, so while riding down busy Army Post Road in Des Moines, we "celebrated" the occasion by turning on every knob, button, and lever we could find. Gary actually responded very well to our immature actions, and continued to drive unshaken while the radio blared, the window washers washed, the wipers wiped, the heater blasted in the middle of summer, and the turn signals blinked one direction, then the other.

Yes, I know how foolish that all sounds now, but then it seemed like fun. By the way, this is the very same 1960 white Rambler that Gary's dad crashed into a brand new Corvette while taking us back to college in Ankeny one weekend. I remember standing in the intersection after the crash listening to the fiberglass body on the Vet continue to pop and crack as the damage spread across the front then down the side. The Rambler was barely dented.

We were not in every class together in school, but we were together in a lot of them. Therefore, we shared in a number of incidents (memories) that we recall to this day. There was the short substitute teacher that did not know how to use the intercom system. When receiving a call during a class, we told her she needed to speak directly into the black button which was a good 10 inches above her head. She pulled over a chair and stood on it in order to speak into that button, but of course, the little button had nothing to do with responding to the call. She eventually went to the office to check out the call, and while she was gone, the classroom door mysteriously locked behind her.

When she returned, she found her class in deep concentration on their studies, so deep they could not hear her knocking on the door to get in. And when she returned in a few minutes with the Principal to unlock the door, she found it had, just as mysteriously, unlocked itself. Yes, I ought to be ashamed of myself for letting such a situation take place, but I remember it was all Gary's idea – at least that is what I told the Principal when he called me into his office.

One school morning I remember Gary coming into a class laughing. I wanted in on the joke, so I said, "What's going on?" Gary explained that while driving to school that morning he had sneezed, and just now upon visiting the men's room, came to the realization that he had a big booger sticking on the neck of his T-shirt where everyone could see it! Apparently, it looked somewhat like a broach sticking right there in the front of his neckline. Now, that is funny. Yea, I know, some of you do not think so.

One day in Mrs. Brady's Spanish class I decided to play a trick on Gary. Spanish class was always fun, especially when we used headphones to listen to tapes. The people on the tapes would make a statement, then we would repeat it. You could kind of go at your own speed. I also liked that approach to learning because if you played with your headset button, you could tune into KIOA radio and listen to songs. Those songs were just written, and now they are "the oldies!"

I had just one piece of gum left in my pocket. I figured if I tried to "sneak chew" it, Gary would tell on me, and I'd get into trouble. So, I reached in my pocket and pretended to put something into my mouth, and occasionally pretended to sneak a chew or two. Gary saw me chewing and immediately said to me, "Give me some of whatever that is, or I will tell

Mrs. Brady on you." Back in our day, chewing gum in school was a capital offense punishable before a firing squad. After all, "If you kids had to scrape the gum off the bottom of the desks, you would know how much of a problem it is!"

I reached in my pocket, grabbed the last piece of gum, and gave it to him. I mean what are friends for? He craftily put it in his mouth, and as soon as he did, I raised my hand and said, "Mrs. Brady, I believe Gary Rothfus is chewing gum, and I know that is against the rules." Gary then responded, "Jim is chewing gum too, Mrs. Brady," but of course, I wasn't, and I showed her I had nothing in my mouth. That went off so smoothly, I was quite proud of myself! After that, no one would take any edible substance from me for fear of the same thing happening to them. Do you see why I had very few friends?

There was one other occasion in school where I actually did have something in my mouth and got caught. I will prepare you beforehand by letting you know that I realize not everyone prefers to chew on the same things. I, for one, happened to like green olives with the seeds in them (a rare find today). And when I was done eating the olive, I, for some neurotic reason, liked to keep the big seed in my mouth and sort of just play with it in there.

One morning as I left for school I popped two big green olives in my mouth. Around 10:00am I entered Miss Lawson's English class with those two seeds still rattling around in there. Midway through class she must have noticed that it appeared like I had something in my mouth, so she said to me, "Mr. Garnett, do you have candy in your mouth?" I said, "No." She said, "Mr. Garnett, do you have gum in your mouth?" I said, "No." She then said, "Mr. Garnett, what is it that you have in your mouth?" I replied, "Two olive seeds."

I am not sure why that answer caused my fellow

students to look at me the way they did, but you would have thought I would have just confessed to eating glass light bulbs!

Miss Lawson then said, "Mr. Garnett, please come up here and put whatever is in your mouth into the waste basket!" I walked to the front of the room, looked down at the wastebasket and knew I was in trouble – the mental wastebasket was completely empty! These two olive seeds were going to make a really loud noise when they hit the bottom of that metal wastebasket – and they certainly did! It sounded like two canons on Memorial Day! Now, if I had been a shy introverted student, that would have scared me for life, but instead, when everyone in the room broke into laughter (I think I saw a little smile on Miss Lawson's face), I actually felt good about the whole deal. I did know enough not to try that twice in her class though.

Mentioning Miss Lawson brings a smile to my face. She was tall and wore her red hair stacked high on her head. I imagine there was a name for that style, but I think you get the idea. She was a "class act" with numerous pairs of glasses to match her different outfits. She also was an excellent teacher. In fact, I wrote Miss Lawson 25 years after I graduated college, and told her she was one of the best teachers I had. Her lessons prepared me, not only for college, but also for a career of speaking and writing.

Anyway, back to Gary. Gary "stored" all his homework assignments in his notebook. He did not have it organized into any type of a system or anything, but he knew "it was in there somewhere." Would you get the picture if I said his notebook resembled a pile of papers that were in total disarray? Absolute, total chaos.

On more than one occasion, Miss Lawson stood next to Gary's desk waiting for him to give her his homework assignment. He knew he had it but just wasn't sure where. He was an A student, but that did not make him organized. Miss Lawson's face would sooner-than-later start to turn red (to match her red hair), and she would present her lecture to him on keeping things organized. Although, Miss Lawson did not think our laughter was the least bit appropriate, it was hard to contain! I don't know how Gary ever passed her class – not because of his grades, but because of her death threats!

I could tell you about other things Gary and I did, like play penny-poker with the guys in my bedroom. That was a good place to play because the mirror on my dresser tipped downward, showing the rest of us Gary's cards. I am not sure he ever caught on to why his "luck" was not good.

Some of you may be thinking that I played a lot of pranks on Gary, but you need to understand we all played a lot of pranks on each other. I was recipient to as many tricks as everyone else, and I learned quickly that if one was going to "dish it out," he must also learn to "take it in!"

For instance, in my junior year, just before school was dismissed for the summer, we were to turn in our class books to our respective teachers. I could not find my World History book, and that class was taught by one of my favorite teachers, Coach Bankus. I simply could not find it. Finally, in desperation, I approached him and told him I could not find the book. He said, "Someone must have found it and turned it in for you. I have it right here. I have been waiting to speak to you about it."

With that, he handed me my book. It had a section of pages that had been stapled together, and in between the staples was an open-faced, honey butter sandwich.

Apparently, whoever did this dastardly deed stapled their finger in the process because there was blood all over the pages.

Mr. Bankus said, "I'm afraid this book is no good to anyone. It is going to cost you $6.50." I thought at first he was joking, but it was no joke! In those days, $6.50 was a lot of money to pay for anything – let alone a schoolbook!

Before the day was over, Ronnie Wyckoff asked me if I ever found my World History book, and by the way he asked, I knew he was the culprit. I had to admit though, that it was a pretty funny thing to do to someone. I would have done it to him had I thought of it.

So, now you understand how the game was played among my friends and me. Yeah, I know, with friends like that, who needs enemies – there may be some truth in that!

We even made a pact to buy each other Christmas gifts one year, but then decided not to. No one ever informed Gary about the decision not to, so he got us all gifts. Now that was funny!

Gary and I do not see each other much anymore. As happens, as you grow older, you see your friends at the funerals of your parents.

Gary played an instrumental roll in creating so many good memories in my childhood. And the funny thing about it - we never knew that we were creating memories. We were just two "gourd head" kids enjoying our youth and living life as it came to us. Those were the days.

Do you recall me saying that Gary and I were such good friends, that if I were to phone him and call him a "gourd head," he would know exactly what I meant? Well, I decided to do just that, and you know what? He had no idea what I was talking about! In fact, as I shared many of the incidents in this chapter with him, he only had a vague recollection of them! I asked him if he had just suffered a stroke.

Then my precious wife explained to me that these are **my** memories of our friendship, not his. He has his own, most likely of the ones where I look like an idiot and he looked good!

Chapter Thirty-Five

One Summer Night At The Drive-In Theater

One summer Saturday night in 1966 someone suggested that we should go to the drive-in movie in Des Moines at the 14th Street Drive-In Theater. So, five of us guys decided to pile in my car and go.

I had recently purchased that 1954, black-and-white, 4-door Ford for $50.00. I quickly changed it to an all-black 1954 Ford by spray-painting the white trunk black. In doing so, I got black paint overspray on the back window that took more time to remove than the other paint did to apply.

For those of you who have never been to a drive-in movie, imagine a large parking lot the size of a football field, with individual parking spaces. To the left of each parking was a window-height pole that held the speaker that space allowed you to hear the movie. You unhooked the speaker from the pole and clipped it to the inside of your partially rolled down driver's window. It actually worked pretty well.

The 14th Street Drive-In Theatre In Des Moines.

At the front of the parking lot was a huge, smooth white wall that served as the movie "screen." Depending on the venue, this screen could be as large as 150' X 200'. It could be made out of concrete, wood, or metal. It just had to reflect well. Remember, we were not privy to such things as High Definition back then, so when you only have Low Definition to compare everything to, it looked pretty good. One could park at the rear of the parking lot and be some 250' away, and still see the picture fine.

There was a real novelty in going to a drive-in movie in the summer. The movie could not begin until it was sufficiently dark, so you arrived while it was still light, then waited for it to be dark enough to begin. While it was light, families that went together would often sit outside in lawn chairs and enjoy goodies from their picnic basket. I guess it was kind of like tailgating before a football game. Once it started to get dark, though, people would get back into their cars.

You may wonder why five guys would go to a drive-in movie together. Although drive-in movies eventually earned the reputation of being for guys and their gals, it was not limited to couples. If you went with your buddies, you did not have to be careful about things like belching out loud after drinking your Pepsi (made with pure sugar, nonetheless), or dropping mustard on your shirt, or passing gas. Sometimes with your buddies, you could even hold contests as to who could belch or pass gas the loudest. But basically, the main advantage was simply that it was cheaper!

That summer night we chose to take my 1954 Ford to the double feature. We were aware that some moviegoers would hide in the trunk of the car to avoid purchasing tickets, but we did not think that would be the honorable thing to do, so all five of us paid.

The first movie was pretty good, but by the time the intermission came, everyone was hungry and thirsty. For some reason, no one wanted to go to the concession stand, so we drew straws, and the shortest one went to Larry Newman. Larry was a good guy and a good friend, even though you may recall he was the classmate that hit me in the leg with a golf ball and stunted my golfing career.

We all wrote down our orders, gave our monies to Larry, and watched him go inside the concession stand. He had not been inside for 10 seconds when the thought occurred to me that it would be funny to move the car while he was ordering, then watch his reaction when he returned to find us gone.

So, I carefully backed my car up two rows so we could see him but so he could not see us. Then we watched as he return with our food and drinks to find only an empty space where our car used to be parked. He was stunned! It was a perfectly executed prank! We were laughing, clapping our hands, and patting ourselves on the back..

That is, until Larry decided to take advantage of the fact that he was alone with all of our food. Larry was a trusting soul, but he was not stupid. After he realized what we had done, he began to unwrap the sandwiches and sample each. He had turned the trick on us! I started the car immediately and slowly pulled back up into the same space where we were previously parked. Then we all jumped out and grabbed our food before Larry could devour it all!

Things like this happened to us all the time – the prank would backfire, and someone other than the intended target would get the worst of it! But that was okay because it was funny too. I guess, looking back, that was really all we were after – something to make us laugh, something to keep us from being bored, something to make us appreciate the fact that life was good!

Sharon Holder's 7th Grade Class
We were together the day John F. Kennedy was assassinated.
(Cousin Susie and I are back row 2nd and 3rd from right)

Chapter Thirty-Six

The Annual Pilgrimage To See The Most Feared Person Of My Childhood

Once a year the three Garnett children were taken on a pilgrimage to Des Moines to see the most feared person of my childhood- the dentist. Even though it meant getting out of school for one whole afternoon, I would have given anything to be allowed to stay in school and miss the journey. But no amount of complaining, crabbing, or crying would excuse me from the journey.

The dentist's name was Dr. Davis, and he worked in the Equitable Building in downtown Des Moines. My family chose him because his assistant was our aunt Gale Foulk. She was really nice, and I liked her, but I certainly wish she had chosen another profession. After making the visit, we would brag to our friends that we had just been in the "tallest building in Des Moines!" We thought that would make them more envious than telling them we had gone to the dentist.

Mom did not drive back then, but even if she had, we only had one car, and Dad drove it to work. This was the common scenario in the 1950's - one driver and one car per family. That was "the normal" and did not seem like an inconvenience to us. But then, a lot of things did not seem like an inconvenience in the 50's until later when they turned into necessities – like air conditioning and color TV.

The pilgrimage would begin by walking from our house to "Charlie's Station" on the corner of 5th Street and Highway 5. An older man by the name of Charlie owned this store that sat back off the highway just far enough for the Greyhound bus to pull in and pick up passengers who had purchased a ticket to Des Moines.

While we waited for the bus to come (and believe me, my mom was always extremely early), we would occupy ourselves by peering into Charlie's display cases that were filled with candy. Most of it was only a nickel or less, but that was a lot of money then. Once in a while Mom would let us buy some candy, but we had to wait to eat it until after we had seen the dentist. I suppose it would not have been right to have him see the Snicker's on your teeth when he examined you.

I remember the smell of that big Greyhound bus, but later realized the smell was actually that of diesel fuel. The smell was even stronger when we got off at the bus station. From the bus station we walked a number of blocks to the Equitable Building that was located on 6th and Locust. It seemed like a long way to a little boy, but it was exciting – or at least *would have been* had we not been going to the dentist!

 The last "fun part" of the trip was taking the elevator up to his office. From there on, I began to get scared. You see, my mom used that common 1950's parenting technique when we were naughty. That was the technique where you told your children that if they did not "straighten up," they would have to go to the doctor and get a shot! I do not know where that technique originated, but for the short term, it really worked. Unfortunately, for the long term it made kids hate doctors – and dentists pretty much forever.

My mouth was not a stranger to cavities, so of course, this annual visit usually showed up some problem that needed to be fixed. I would be given the option of having Novocain, but of course it is administered with a needle and a syringe – in other words, "a shot." I got a glimpse of that needle once while he was trying to hide behind his back. It was the size of a needle you would use on a horse! I wanted no part of it, so, I chose to go it without Novocain.

Can you imagine having a tooth fixed with no numbing? Rather barbaric, even for the 1950's! It was extremely painful and frightening to a little boy! I would rate it right up there with torture in a concentration camp. Of course, my Aunt Gail was right there to hold my hand, but I never found her holding my hand to compensate for the pain in my jaw! I cried, and jerked, and screamed, and did everything I could to get sympathy from the doctor, but nothing worked. It seemed like I spent days in his chair.

After having my first cavity fixed, I would cry at the very mention of the word "dentist." I absolutely hated it! It was like anticipating sticking your finger in an electrical outlet.

When the frightful ordeal in the chair was finally over, the doctor offered a big box of prizes that you could pick from. Let me tell you, there was not a prize in that box that was worth the torture I had endured in his chair. The experience was definitely a life-changer! I am sure that I never chose the luxury of Novocain until several years of dentist visits. When I received my first injection, I was simply amazed that it did not hurt much as I thought it would. I could not believe that once the shot was over, there was no pain. Now I would choose to do it differently if I could, but of course there is no "rewind" button for life.

Amid my screams for mercy, I also remember a little white porcelain sink just to the left of the dentist chair. Water continually spiraled in this white sink the purpose of which was to discard (spit) all the gunk that accumulated in your mouth while he was working on you. I would have loved to play with that swirling water had circumstances been different.

After leaving the dentist's office, we would walk a number of blocks to the south side of the downtown business district. Dad worked at a place called The Des Moines Drug Company that supplied pharmacies with their drugs.

It was always late afternoon when we arrived at Dad's place of work. After a short time, we would hear a buzzer sound that signaled the end of the workday. Within a few minutes, the employees would begin filing down the stairs one-by-one to where we were waiting by the front door. We would see Pete, who was usually one of the first to come down, then Dale and his brother Charlie, then my dad.

It was always so exciting to see him! It was much neater than just seeing him at home when he returned from work. This was where he spent all day, doing what whatever he did to provide for his family. I was so proud of him and would point out to anyone who was watching, that the guy coming down the stairs was "my dad."

The annual trek to see the most feared person of my childhood certainly made a lasting impression on me. If I could have eliminated the pain from the trip, it would have been something I looked forward to, rather than dreaded. But in the eyes of a little boy, there was nothing scarier than the thought of having that big horse needle rammed into my mouth.

I am sure there is a lesson to be learned in all that. Maybe something like "the things we most fear can actually be a blessing in disguise." But then, I was just a little boy, and was not much into learning life's lessons at my young age.

Chapter Thirty-Seven

The Carlisle Cemetery
(Where Names Became Real People)

Although this situation took place in my life when I was an adult, it had to do with information I was given all during my childhood years. You will understand what I mean as you continue reading.

My dad, Lyle Garnett, often talked about growing up in Carlisle. He was apparently quite a good athlete, and as such played on a number of different types of athletic teams. Baseball and basketball were the two he talked about the most.

I remember one time Dad told us that he played on a town basketball team that had beaten the world-famous Harlem Globetrotters. I thought he was just pulling our legs, that is, until he produced a newspaper clipping that showed the picture of his team and verified his claim.

Anyway, as Dad talked about playing sports and doing other things (like stealing watermelons from someone's patch in Avon Lake), he would relay the names of his friends that were involved in these things with him.

As Dad talked about his friends, he seemed to forget that I did not know them and had never met them. He would refer to Glen, Stuffy, Red, Arden, and George and talk about what they did together or where they lived or who their sister was that he had dated.

I remember one time he told me a lady's name, like I had any idea who she was, and said he bought her a whole box of stationery with flowered envelopes. He had hopes of dating her. But before he gave the box of stationary to her, he addressed all the envelopes to himself! I thought that was simply genius! I guess he did not receive any letters from her at all.

For years I heard about his childhood friends until I actually knew some of their characteristics. But again, I had never met any of them, and to me, they were just names.

Then the day came that I drove to the Carlisle Cemetery to visit my dad's grave. He died in 2001. As I left his gravesite, I drove slowly through the cemetery and was absolutely startled.

I saw on one of the headstones a name that my dad had referred to so often. A bit further down the lane, I saw another name, then another, then another. Seeing those names etched there on their gravestones, made them "come alive" to me. I had heard all about these people from my dad, but because I did not know them, they were just names to me. But here they were, their names on their headstones verified that they were real people – real people whom my dad had known personally. He had lived with them, laughed with them, loved them, and most likely stood on the edge of their grave and wept for them at their death. They were my dad's friends.

I had seen what some of them looked like in old pictures, and I could begin to piece together the life that they enjoyed, and the small part that my dad played in their life at a given time.

That trip to the cemetery that afternoon had a profound affect on me. It was kind of like the first time I met my elementary teacher's husband, and all of a sudden I saw her as a real person. She had a life away from the classroom where she was part of a real family with ups and downs, laughs and tears, joys and sorrows – real life stuff.

That's how I now saw these people for the first time – Glen, Stuffy, Red, Arden, and George - they were more than names, they were real people.

Entrance into the Carlisle Cemetery

Conclusion

I asked a woman recently if she had ever considered putting her childhood memories down on paper. She looked at me with a bewildered look and said, "Why on earth would I want to do that? I am trying to forget them!" That must be tough to deal with, but apparently that is how some people view their childhood.

Just the opposite is true for me. As I wrote about my childhood memories, I began to realize just how good of a childhood I had.

I view my childhood now from a perspective gained through 65 years of living. I am in a much better position to judge between what is a good childhood and what is a bad childhood. My childhood ranks high on the good list.

"Growing Up Carlisle" in the 50's and 60's was exactly the right place at exactly the right time for me. Looking back, I wouldn't change a day of it!

The Author

Jim Garnett was born in the small Mid-western town of Carlisle, Iowa, November 9, 1949, to Lyle and Sally Garnett. He lived at 650 School Street until he graduated from Carlisle High School in 1968 and moved away for a college education.

After graduating college, Jim served as a Senior Pastor for almost 30 years, then as a financial counselor for 15 years, before retiring in 2011. He has distinguished himself as a sought-after speaker, counselor, educator, and author.

He is now retired and lives in Ankeny, Iowa, with his wife Ginny.

Contact Information
Jim Garnett
Ankeny Iowa
515-577-1799
growingupcarlisle@gmail.com